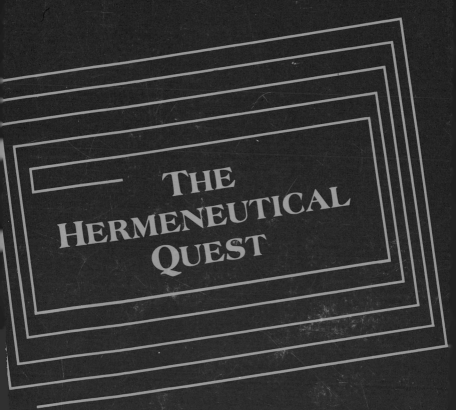

THE HERMENEUTICAL QUEST

Essays in Honor of James Luther Mays
on his Sixty-Fifth Birthday

Edited by
Donald G. Miller

PRINCETON THEOLOGICAL MONOGRAPHS

Series

Dikran Y. Hadidian

General Editor

4

THE HERMENEUTICAL QUEST

Essays in Honor of James Luther Mays
on his Sixty-Fifth Birthday

THE HERMENEUTICAL QUEST

Essays in Honor of James Luther Mays
on his Sixty-Fifth Birthday

Edited by

Donald G. Miller

PICKWICK PUBLICATIONS
Allison Park, Pennsylvania

Copyright © 1986 by **Pickwick Publications**
4137 Timberlane Drive, Allison Park, PA 15101

Library of Congress Cataloging-in-Publication Data
The Hermeneutical Quest

   (Princeton theological monograph series; 4)
   Bibliography: p.
   1. Bible—Hermeneutics—Addresses, essays, lectures.
2. Theology—Addresses, essays, lectures. 3. Mays,
James Luther—Addresses, essays, lectures. I. Mays,
James Luther. II. Miller, Donald G. III. Series:
Princeton theological monograph series; 4.
BS476.H466 1986   220.6'01 86-833
ISBN 0-915138-86-7

Printed and Bound by Publishers Choice Book Mfg. Co.
Mars, Pennsylvania 16046

CONTENTS

FOREWORD

To some it is given to be flamboyant. Like Roman candles, they light up the sky momentarily as each new fad appears, flaming gloriously as nine-day wonders, then spurt and fizzle until their next effete explosion. Their final legacy is a memory of brief excitement and a few burned out spots on the landscape. Others run deeper. Like the quiet dignity of the incoming tide or the noiseless rising of the sun, they do their work with power and leave a lasting deposit of warmth and light on the landscape of their endeavors. Without ostentation or self-glorification, they give themselves to lives of quiet thoughtfulness and disciplined toil, leaving to their fellow creatures a heritage of truth and values to guide and nurture generations yet to come.

Of the latter type is James Luther Mays. Following his undergraduate study and three years of active service in the Air Force during World War II, he has spent four decades as a graduate student, pastor in both rural and town churches, professor, Fulbright lecturer in Germany, editor of the quarterly journal *Interpretation* and two series of books, author of several volumes of lasting value, churchman, stimulating colleague and friend. It is fitting that he should be honored on his sixty-fifth birthday by this volume of essays. The list of contributors could have been lengthened indefinitely, but to keep the book within limits only Old Testament scholars were invited to write, with two exceptions for special reasons, and only a very select group of them.

In a statement not intended for publication but written in correspondence with a friend, James Mays himself set the theme of the volume. He wrote:

> "What should be the fundamental and directive hermeneutical question brought to the text in the biblical interpretation that is taught in seminaries and practiced in the church?. . . to my mind it is the question that needs to be thought about seriously when seminary curricula are planned, courses designed, and all the projects of biblical interpretation for preaching and teaching in the church carried out."

This statement, in somewhat longer form, was sent to all the contributors as a guide to their choice of subjects for the volume. The writers were also asked, where possible, to relate the hermeneutical themes with which they dealt to issues current in the theological world. In this way, the volume has been given a unity of theme and a relation to contemporary subjects not always present in a collection of essays by different authors.

John H. Leith, a former college mate of James Mays and a present colleague, gives us a personal appreciation of him from the standpoint of one who has known him most of his lifetime.

James Barr deals with the broad, comprehensive demands which "theological" exegesis imposes upon biblical scholarship, then applies his thought critically to both the Old and the New Quest for the historical Jesus. He contrasts what is often held to be "theological" exegesis, the bringing of a prior theology to the text, and genuine "theological" exegesis which allows the text to challenge the theologies brought to it, and influence, enrich and modify them.

Claus Westermann shows how biblical thought avoids mere ideas and speculations, and always deals with reality, whether it be in the creation stories, the patriarchal accounts, the prophets, the psalms, the wisdom writers or the parables of Jesus, and points out the interpretive significance of this for the contemporary church, summoning the church to abandon its abstract, theoretical language for the concrete realities which confront humankind both in the Bible and in their lives.

Ronald S. Clements presents a reassessment of the effort to discover behind written prophecy the original oral content which it sought to preserve, a reassessment necessitated by the rise of canon criticism and redaction criticism. He affirms that the formation of the written prophetic canon in its fixed form had theological significance in the developing faith of Israel, and suggests some ways in which this is to be understood today.

Brevard S. Childs appraises approvingly the contribution Gerhard von Rad made to the theological understanding of the biblical witness but notes a weakness in von Rad's failure to see the theological and exegetical importance of the formation of the canon, which has opened the door for succeeding scholars to champion a process of development which tends to negate the decisive and final revelation of God in Jesus Christ.

Roland E. Murphy raises the question why the Book of Proverbs has been subjected to a theological "benign neglect" and almost decanonized, then proceeds to develop a theology of Proverbs based on Israel's experience of God as the essential dimension of reality for them, and the personification of the figure of Lady Wisdom as "the Lord's self-revelation through creation."

Elizabeth Achtemeier brands the church's discrimination against women as "a scandal to the gospel of Jesus Christ," and calls for a new affirmation in action of the freedom that women have been given through the gospel. She brings into question, however, the almost universal demand of feminist theologians to use female language for God. This she finds wholly unacceptable in the light of the biblical revelation, and fears that if we create a theology out of experience rather than the Word of God, the feminist movement in the church could lead to a denial of the gospel even worse than that from which it seeks to deliver us.

F. Wellford Hobbie's article was his last piece of creative work produced before his untimely death. A classmate of James Mays and a faculty colleague for the past eleven years, he had capitalized on James's strong interest in preparing students to interpret the Scriptures properly through the pulpit by commandeering him on occasion as a "team teacher" in courses on Homiletics. In this article he gives some of the fruit of that common endeavor in an analysis of the hermeneutical process involved in sermon preparation.

Patrick D. Miller, a former colleague of James Mays, proposes the theme of God as sovereign as "the foundation stone of both Old Testament and Reformed theology," then lifts up three primary images—God as King, Judge and Warrior—as Old Testament vehicles for presenting this truth. The hermeneutical significance of these is that they are not mere human metaphors to quicken the imagination about God, but are controlling features in the life and thought of Israel as they developed their faith in God as the divine governor both of history and of the universe.

James A. Sanders raises the question of the proper relation of the theological seminaries to the believing communities, and suggests clues to an answer through his own concept of canonical criticism as outlined in some of his books. He views the canon not as a fixed body of documents selected by the ancient church as authoritative over all subsequently developing tradition, but rather as a paradigm, in its "pluralistic richness," for the church's pilgrimage in every generation. He suggests that its categories of pilgrim, witness, servant and steward should guide both seminaries and congregations in their search for the wholeness of truth in our time, by an ongoing monotheizing process which will destroy all current idolatries.

Paul D. Hanson expresses wholehearted approval of the current effort to remove gender-biased language from our speaking about God and one another in the church's worship and life, and gives his reasons for so doing. He raises a caution, however, concerning the recent attempt of the *Inclusive-Language Lectionary*, making a clear distinction between the *interpretation* of biblical writings and their *translation*. He argues that a translation should be faithful to the historical meaning of the text, and that "the dynamic, progressive quality of biblical faith is blurred by attempts to remove historical/cultural-specific aspects."

John B. Trotti, a colleague of James Mays, has prepared a complete bibliography of his writings, arranged in the chronological order of their appearance.

It is plain from these essays that there is at present no unanimity of judgment about the task of interpreting the meaning of Scripture for our time, and that the hermeneutical quest is by no means over. Trends are currently in a state of flux. An interchange of opinion such as is here represented, however, is a part of the process by which progress into the future may be made.

This volume is presented as a tribute to Professor Mays in the hope that it will be a worthy stimulus to genuine theological interpretation of the Scriptures to which he has devoted his career.

Donald G. Miller
Former teacher, colleague and abiding friend of James Mays.

James Luther Mays
by John H. Leith

James Luther Mays was invited to teach at Union Theological Seminary in 1955. This invitation established his calling in biblical studies and placed him in an Old Testament department which had been given distinction by John Bright. The persistence and the devotion with which James Mays has fulfilled his calling is characteristic of his personality. The action of President Benjamin Rice Lacy in seeking out James Mays from the pastorate and bringing him to Union Theological Seminary has now culminated in twenty-nine years of teaching theological students and in his election as the president of the Society of Biblical Literature in 1985.

James Mays was born in Louisville, Georgia on July 14, 1921. His father, Allen Mays, was the son of an established farmer in the Louisville community. One of James Mays' best memories is visits to his grandfather's home and farm. He once openly expressed his anguish when on a visit to Louisville, Georgia he found all evidences of the farm erased by the tree planting of a paper company. His mother, Ruth Irene Mosteller, was from North Carolina, moving from Hickory to Louisville in 1918. The Mostellers were Lutheran and Holshousers were German Reformed. James Mays was told very early in life that his grandfather, Luther Mosteller had been called home from seminary to assume responsibilities on his father's farm and that he wanted his grandson to fulfill the vocation which had been denied him. The extent to which human freedom and self-determination modify the heritage of family and the social matrix of community is much debated. However, there can be little doubt on the part of those who know him that all three factors are significant in James May's own development. According to his own faith the personal, social, physical factors which shaped the life of James Mays have to be set in the more basic context of the Divine Providence and Election about which he has taught and preached and which can be discerned only by faith.

Louisville, Georgia was a small southern town situated in an area that has been celebrated by Erskine Caldwell's novels. The poverty which Caldwell depicted was true enough and was pervasive throughout the South. The impact of living in the South during the 1930s left its mark on all persons who experienced the depression. The story which James Mays related in a chapel service at

Union Theological Seminary testified to the vivid imprint on his memory of the human reality of those years. It was Christmastime and he had secured a job sacking groceries in a local store. One day a young white boy from the country came in with his brogans, his overalls, a ragged denim shirt and a heavily knit sweater. He pressed his face against the window of the store looking in at the fruit and Christmas food for which he had no money to buy. The poignancy of this scene was obvious to Jim Mays, to another clerk and to the owner of the grocery store who picked up a bag of oranges and rushed out and gave it to the boy as he was leaving. The putting of this story into writing destroys its poignancy; in the original setting the human reality was communicated without words in the context of a common human experience.

The tobacco road literature, however, failed to communicate the existence of very strong and powerful cultural traditions that maintained human dignity in the midst of poverty and adversity. Louisville was a southern town with a Scotch-Irish culture. This culture had placed a premium on human dignity and self-responsibility, even in the midst of or perhaps especially in the midst of poverty and adversity. Other characteristics of this culture were a great sense of reality, an abhorrence of the ostentatious, the pretentious, the pompous, the contrived and the artificial. This culture placed value upon self-determination, upon personal privacy and dignity, upon consistency and integrity of action.

The religious heritage into which James Mays was born was Presbyterian, though his mother had a Lutheran background. The Presbyterian community had existed in Louisville at least from the 1790s. The particular form of Presbyterianism into which James Mays was born was that of the Associate Reformed Presbyterian Church. The Associates and the Reformed were secessionist churches from the Church of Scotland. The experience of withdrawal from the Church of Scotland had also been tempered for most of the Associates and the Reformed in America by life in northern Ireland before their emigration.

The secessionist churches were both more radical and more conservative. They were less influenced by the general culture than Presbyterians generally. The Associate Reformed Presbyterian Church, for example, continued the tradition of exclusive psalmody until 1946. It also maintained a strong Sabbatarian influence which had developed among the Puritan Presbyterians in Britain. More than most churches, up until the 1940s, the Associate Reformed Presbyterians as a small group had maintained the integrity of their ancient heritage from dilution in the American culture better than Presbyterians generally.

Louisville was also a center of culture. It had been the capital of Georgia during the period 1795-1804. The existence of the capital had left an aristocratic leadership tradition. It had also left a strong cultural tradition that centered in the school system. The Louisville Academy had been chartered in 1796 by the University of Georgia School System. This academy emphasized classical and liberal learning. It later became part of the public school system of Georgia, but when James Mays was a student it still was informed by this long-established cultural tradition. William L. Pressly, who served as president of Westminister Schools and as president of Southern Association of Schools and Colleges, had grown up in the Louisville community in the decade before the birth of James Mays. He has attested the unusually high quality and the emphasis on classical learning which were maintained in the school and which prepared students for careers in the best educational institutions in America. This emphasis of an institution committed to classical learning, to teaching students to read and to discriminate among values, to analyze and to reflect critically upon data and events had a lasting impression upon James Mays as well as other young people who left Louisville for distinguished careers.

The character of the school is reflected in the unusual qualifications of the faculty who taught James Mays in high school. Moffatt Plaxco was pastor of the Associate Reformed Presbyterian Church and also superintendent of the school. He had received an excellent education: an A.B. degree from Erskine College, Bachelor of Divinity degrees from Erskine and Princeton Theological Seminaries. He also held an M.A. degree from Princeton University. In the Louisville Academy he taught Latin and senior literature.

Mrs. Herschel E. Smith, another teacher in the Louisville Academy, was an A.B. graduate of Wellesley and had done graduate work at the University of Grenoble and at the Sorbonne. Other teachers were Raiford McMillan who had degrees from Clemson College and Erskine College; Charles Cofer with degrees from Erskine College and the University of Georgia; Mrs. Frank Hardiman with degrees from Wesleyan College and Georgia State College at Millédgeville.

The culture in which James Mays grew up with its peculiar Scotch-Irish emphases and its union of classical learning with piety represented Presbyterian influence at its best. Such a culture no longer exists except perhaps in very isolated spots and without this culture such persons as James Mays will be increasingly rare.

James Mays entered Erskine College in 1938. Erskine was a liberal arts institution of the Associate Reformed Presbyterian Church. It attempted to unite piety and learning, but it suffered under the incredible poverty of most institutions in the South during that period. Its library actually numbered 12,000 or fewer volumes. Its professors were distinguished by their personal qualities but not by their intellectual attainments. Yet in a remarkable way it did represent cultural intregity and dignity and a commitment both to piety and learning.

One of the strongest characteristics of Erskine College at that time was a student body composed of persons who had similar backgrounds to James Mays. While at Erskine, James Mays distinguished himself not only as a scholar but as a participant in many campus activities. He was a member of the Garnet Circle which was limited to the 20 students with the highest academic records. He was also active in music and a member of the Glee Club for four years. He sang in the Octet for three years. His senior year he was editor of the college annual.

James Mays was especially active in forensic affairs. He participated in debate and won the state debating tournament his junior year. He was a member of the Philomathean Literary Society and was a winner of the annual debate between the Philomatheans and the Euphemians, also his junior year. The importance of this kind of forensic activity is documented by the number of distinguished Presbyterian ministers whose names appear on the debate trophy which lists the winners of the annual Philomathean-Euphemian commencement debate.

James Mays developed an increasing interest in philosophy and in critical reflection while a student at Erskine. He was influenced by Professor Harold J. Ralston who held degrees from Princeton University and Iowa University. Harold Ralston was later professor at Monmouth College and a member of the Board of Trustees at Pittsburgh Theological Seminary. At Erskine he taught a wide variety of courses including Bible, psychology, and philosophy. During James Mays' years at Erskine there was an overwhelming pressure for good students to major in science and then become medical doctors. Over against the urging of at least one prominent faculty member, James Mays declared himself for the liberal arts. There is a rumor that he enjoyed raising critical philosophical and historical questions for the discomfort of students at the Erskine Theological Seminary.

James Mays married Mary Will Boyd, his college sweetheart, on August 23, 1943. She was from Covington, Tennessee, a town with similarities to Louisville. Her father was a ruling Elder and church school superintendent in the Associate Reformed Presbyterian Church. Two uncles were ministers: John L. Boyd in the Associate Reformed Presbyterian Church and Charles M. Boyd, a minister in the Presbyterian Church U.S. whose pastorates included the First Presbyterian Church, Tuscaloosa, Alabama. The Mays have two children, Sarah Mays Rogerson of Los Angeles, California and Mary Frances Mays of Richmond.

Military experience followed his college work. He spent the years 1942-45 in the United States Air Force and the Air Transport Command. He was in the Pacific, American and European theaters and received four battle stars and the Air Medal. These were influential years in developing a keen sense for reality, a vision of how large the world is and of the true context in which our parochial lives must be lived.

The year following military service was spent at Columbia University studying philosophy. This, as has been indicated, was an interest from college days, but as a student at Columbia University he became aware that philosophy lacked the vitality of theology, that his real vocation was in theology and in the church. Hence, in 1946 James Mays came to Union Theological Seminary. He was an independent student who thought for himself. He did not exactly fit the Union Theological Seminary mold in that era. Yet he distinguished himself as a scholar.

As a student at Union Theological Seminary, James Mays had preached at Mt. Carmel Church in Steeles Tavern, Virginia and on graduation received a call there. On April 19, 1949 at the meeting of Lexington Presbytery in Bethel Church, Staunton, Virginia he was examined for ordination. His sermon on Acts 8:30 was approved. On August 7, 1949 at 8 p.m. he was ordained to the Christian ministry. The sermon was preached by Rev. Charles M. Boyd, D.D. of Mecklenburg Presbytery, an uncle of Mary Will Boyd, his wife.

The Mt. Carmel Church was situated between the Blue Ridge and the Allegheny Mountains. Here James Mays' love of the rural, of nature generally, of bird watching, and of fishing was nurtured. It also is reasonable to assume that this old congregation with deep Presbyterian commitments and biblical knowledge was a very suitable context in which James Mays could develop as a pastor and as a church theologian.

The pastorate at Mt. Carmel was interrupted for a year of study, 1951-52, at the University of Basel. The impact of this year on James Mays was considerable. It placed him in the presence of theologians who commanded his respect, especially of Karl Barth; and it gave him a knowledge of such seminal thinkers as Rudolf Bultmann. The impact of Karl Barth on James Mays was very considerable and was still pronounced when he began teaching at Union Theological Seminary.

James Mays was accompanied to Basel and Palestine by Union Theological Seminary friends, including Wellford Hobbie. He also developed new friendships which would be very influential later. Brevard Childs who is now a professor of Old Testament at Yale University and James Barr who is professor of Hebrew at Oxford University became close friends.

James Mays accepted a call to the First Presbyterian Church in Lincolnton, North Carolina in 1954. Members of the Mt. Carmel congregation at the meeting of Lexington Presbytery on March 12 expressed their appreciation of James Mays and their reluctance in concurring with his request. Presbytery granted the request, and he was dismissed to Kings Mountain Presbytery effective April 1, 1954. On Sunday, May 23, 1954 James Mays was installed as pastor of the First Presbyterian Church of Lincolnton with Fred Stair of Concord Presbytery preaching the sermon. This was to be a very short pastorate of 14 months and was terminated on June 30, 1955 when James Mays accepted a call to Union Theological Seminary.

The call to Union Theological Seminary was presented to James Mays by Dr. Benjamin Rice Lacy, the President of the seminary. Dr. Lacy was determined that the new professor of Old Testament should have a demonstrated competence as a pastor of the church as well as competence for learning. He gave the call to James Mays to come to Union Theological Seminary as both the call of the church and of God to the critically important task of training persons to be pastors of Presbyterian Churches.

The call to Union Theological Seminary brought James Mays into close association with John Bright, one of the most distinguished Old Testament scholars of the twentieth century. Professor Bright says that James Mays was chosen to be his colleague because of his promise of scholarly competence, of judicious temperament, of critical capacities to examine in an objective way the data that were laid before him.

The call to teach Old Testament at Union Theological Seminary required special preparation as James Mays had not planned to be an Old Testament scholar. It is interesting to speculate whether he would himself have chosen to be a professor of Old Testament or would have chosen another field. It is significant that the call to teach Old Testament was not the result of career planning but came as the calling of the church through its agency, Union Theological Seminary. The Seminary made arrangements for James Mays to study under Professor Harold H. Rowley who was an active churchman and a professor at the University of Manchester. Rowley was an outstanding Old Testament scholar, particularly gifted in the field of bibliography. He had a wide acquaintance not only with Old Testament literature but with theological literature in general. He was also an Old Testament scholar with a new awareness of the message of the Old Testament for our time. The years of study under Professor Rowley not only brought James Mays in contact with a great scholar but also with British culture. He received the Ph.D. degree from the University of Manchester in 1957. The respect which Professor Rowley had for James Mays is attested in Rowley's agreement for Union Theological Seminary to acquire his library in 1969 over the bids of other institutions.

In the fall of 1957 James Mays began his teaching career at Union Theological Seminary. In 1960 he was installed as a full professor. In the 29 years that have elapsed since his coming to Union Seminary, he has taught the following courses:

Pentateuch
Exegesis of the Psalms
Advance Hebrew Reading
Exegesis of Mark
Old Testament I
Genesis and Exodus
Interpretation of the Psalms
Biblical Hermeneutics
Introduction to Literature of the Old Testament
Interpretation of the Wisdom Literature
Preaching the Bible
Old Testament II: the Prophets
Readings: Biblical Theology
Readings: Bible and Theology
Doctrine of Scripture
Ezekiel

With Professor Bright
Advanced Hebrew Exegesis
Introduction to Literature of the Old Testament
Theology and Hermeneutics of the Old Testament

With Professor P.D. Miller
Introduction to Study of the Bible
Basic Bible

With Professor Balmer Kelly
Intertestament Literature

With Professor John H. Leith
Theology of Hope

With Professor Cameron Murchison
Introduction to the Ministry

(Courses taught are listed only once. Some courses were taught repeatedly. Seminars on doctoral level are not listed.)

As a teacher, James Mays has always commanded respect. He demands a high level of achievement and emphasizes the mastery of basic texts that make possible theological reflection in preaching. He has great respect for the responsibility of the minister to interpret and apply the Word of God in preaching, teaching and pastoral care. Hence, he has always insisted that theological students meet the same standards of competence as apply in the best professional schools. He has opposed "social passes" to the ministry.

Professor Mays' own position in Old Testament cannot be designated by any particular motif or membership in any school. His work is characterized by meticulous scholarship, highly methodical work habits, and persistent pursuit of goals. One biblical colleague said that Professor Mays' position in the biblical field is distinguished by its great attention to and respect for the text, by allowing the text to say what it meant in the intention of the author. His work is also marked by judiciousness and caution. A further characteristic is attention to blocks of material, paragraphs, themes, books rather than the minute analysis of words, phrases, or sentences. A final distinction is a concern for the meaning of the text for the life of the church today; that is, in particular the meaning of the text for preaching and teaching in the church.

Professor Mays was involved in the work of *Interpretation*

from the time of his arrival as a professor of Old Testament. He became editor of *Interpretation* in 1966 and he maintained this position until 1983. His editorship was very distinguished. Under his leadership, the circulation rose to over ten thousand. As editor he maintained an unusually high standard for theological competence and writing. He secured the allegiance of the best biblical scholars in the world and insisted that they write not for other scholars but for Christian readers generally. The editorship of *Interpretation* was not only a contribution to Christian scholarship and to the work of the church, but it also contributed to the enlargement of Professor Mays' own theological horizon.

In 1966-67 Professor Mays was a Fulbright Lecturer at the University of Goettingen in Germany. Here he had close association with Professor Walther Zimmerli, one of the outstanding Reformed Old Testament scholars in the world. Other distinguished Reformed theologians at Goettingen included Otto Weber, a Barthian and a systematic theologian. In 1964-65 Professor Mays commuted to Pittsburgh to help with the Old Testament courses there.

While maintaining his work as a scholar, teacher, and editor Professor Mays has continued to lecture in theological seminaries and colleges and to preach in churches. He has participated in the Old Testament Colloquium, a group of distinguished Old Testament scholars and in 1985 he was elected president of the Society of Biblical Literature.

Professor Mays is a writer of distinction. He has the unusual capacity to express abstract ideas in intelligible English with clear and precise words and syntax. The logical sequence and the coherence of his thought is always obvious. A bibliography included in this volume lists his published works.

James Mays has also been active in the affairs of the church. He and his family participate in the worship of the Ginter Park Presbyterian Church, and he is a member of Norfolk Presbytery. As a churchman he has served on the Board of Christian Education (1962-1971) and also as chairman and a member of the Committee on Theology and Culture (1973-1979). He has continued to serve on special committees assigned to work on the Presbyterian understanding of the authority of scripture and the nature of revelation.

Every human being made in the image of God is unique, but in Professor Mays the strength of human individuality is obvious. His friends would find it impossible to confuse him with other individuals. He has a remarkable capacity for self-determination, for organizing the energies and vitalities of his life to achieve a deliberately chosen goal, to protect himself from as well as to participate in the affairs of the community. He is not, first of all, a theologian or an Old Testament scholar. He is always, first of all, a human being. The love of creation and participation in the realities of the created world are very important to him. Throughout most of his tenure at Union Seminary he has been an ardent member of the Providence Forge Hunting and Fishing Club. He can live with solitude or with company, in the scholars' study, or hiking in the woods, watching birds or fishing on the lake. To sum it up, James Mays is fundamentally a human being in the presence of the God of the Prophets, the God and Father of our Lord Jesus Christ. He is not consumed by any human enterprise, yet in the service of the church and as a member of the human community he has glorified God and advanced His kingdom.

Exegesis as a Theological Discipline Reconsidered and the Shadow of the Jesus of History

by James Barr

Is exegesis really a theological activity, or can it become one? The question was felt as a central one in the fifties and sixties; it formed a focal point in the interests of the distinguished periodical *Interpretation*, newly founded in Richmond. And no one thought about it more carefully or more responsibly than did James Mays. He was no mere theoretician armed with the latest slogans and avant-garde ideas. His work was done in the midst of the composition of solid and serious commentaries. He was continually concerned with the practical training of students in exegesis and with its outworking in preaching and church life. And, although primarily an Old Testament scholar, he took a keen interest in the exegetical problems of the New. His inaugural lecture at Richmond, delivered in 1960 and entitled "Exegesis as a Theological Discipline," [1] was a model statement of the question as it then presented itself. It was well balanced, excellently written, and informed by a rich classical Christian culture. No single piece of the same length, written within the English-speaking world, seemed to address or to express the issues so well. Thus Mays inaugurated his professorship at Richmond with a statement that for many might well have stood as a fitting monument at the culmination of their career.

Yet he himself would be the first to agree that the question needs to be rethought and restated for today, a quarter of a century later. The passage of that time has seen a great change in the theological situation. In particular, in the sixties "history" was felt to be a central category. It seemed natural to define a central problem area as the conflict between historical study and theological exegesis. On the one hand it was felt that historical study in itself was not theological; on the other hand it might be argued that history, as the milieu of divine action in the world, was itself a theological quantity of great positive importance. However we balance these quantities, the question has now been overtaken by others. Where history then stood, there now stand other quantities, such as literary appreciation and structural analysis. These categories may well dispute the centrality of history; but they do not thereby necessarily support the primacy of theology. The conflict of possibilities has now taken a different shape. And the ideas which were then current under the name of "biblical theology," and the mental atmosphere in which they flourished, can no longer be taken for granted: many of the newer generation have no sense for them.

We may therefore try to look at the question again. In the older approach to the problem, which many of us shared, the question was put thus: taking as starting-point "historical" or "critical" exegesis, we asked how, beginning from this datum, we might move forward to a truly theological exegesis. This way of posing the question appeared to follow naturally from the character of the standard commentaries. These appeared to give the historical and philological data, the background, and perhaps a survey of the exegetical possibilities, but they seemed seldom to advance to the stage of real theological discussion. Granted that these commentaries were serious, responsible and often excellent works, one could take them as a point of departure, but it would then be asked what further steps must be added in order to reach a truly theological level of discussion.

Starting from the existing commentaries, this was a reasonable way to put the question. Translated into a more philosophical mode of expression, the question was often formulated as: Can exegesis be undertaken without theological presuppositions or assumptions? This formulation implied that the mass of exegetical material contained in the commentaries claimed to be independent of theological assumptions; conversely, it was implied that, if it could be shown that theological assumptions were involved in all exegesis, this would alter the character of the exegetical procedures displayed in commentaries and lead towards another kind of exegesis that would be more theologically productive.

The fault in this way of posing the question lay in its starting-point: whatever the starting-point of the commentary may have been, the starting-point of the student in practical study of exegesis is different. The question is not whether we can eventually arrive at theology: the student begins with theology. Theology is there before exegetical knowledge is there. On the whole, people do not build up theological convictions on the basis of exegetical work already done: on the contrary, they have their theological convictions before they do any serious exegetical work. The theological student proceeds from the general to the particular. He knows the centrality of justification by faith before he begins the study of the Pauline letters. He knows the importance of the Virgin Birth before he studies in classroom the evidence of the various Gospels on that subject. He has his view about the historical accuracy of Scripture before he begins to study the differences between Kings and Chronicles. Students do not spend years studying the biblical evidence before they make up their minds whether Paul was right about justification by faith, or whether Jesus was the Son of God in reality. They are sure of the great dogmatic principles before they begin; only because they are sure of these principles do they enter upon the study of theology at all. People's faith is founded upon the general, dogmatic, principles much more than upon the detailed biblical material.

The question then, realistically put, is not how students, having studied exegesis, may advance to becoming theologians: it is rather how, having begun as dogmaticians, they may allow their antecedent dogmatics to be influenced, enriched or modified by the impact of the actual biblical material. If this is the realistic way of putting the question, why has it not generally been expressed in this way? Perhaps we are influenced by the traditional picture of the derivation of theological truth: the Bible is the source, and from it we derive the theological truths. As a general statement this may be correct. But as a matter of educational experience it goes the other way: people learn certain limited dogmatic principles, illustrated by such few texts as appear to support these views, and it is the task of subsequent theological education to make them face the fact that the Bible, or parts of it, may say something apparently different from what they themselves sincerely and passionately believe. Nothing is more difficult for young and active Protestant believers than to learn that the Bible seriously conflicts with even one or two of the principles which they have been brought up to regard as central. The process of such learning is acutely painful and may require long years of agonized inner conflict. Even if the biblical data are quite clear and, at times, unanimous, this does not alleviate the pain. For many people, even if they are fervent believers in biblical authority and inspiration, religious conviction is far more powerful than biblical data. When Scripture is read, religious conviction simply filters out from the conciousness the data, the evidences, the possibilities that seem to conflict with what is already believed to be essential and certain. Thus it is extremely difficult for the actual material of the Bible to overcome the dominion of the inherited theological convictions with which people approach exegesis. This is true not only of beginning students but also of experienced professors.

Thus the practical problem of theological exegesis is not the question of how students, starting with a mass of "nontheological" material, may move on to the higher stage of theological interpretation. It is rather the question of how students who are already deeply convinced of dogmatic positions can come to integrate the biblical material in detail into these positions and in the process, where necessary, make substantial modifications in the positions from which they began. For this the central requisite is the possession of sufficient theological imagination. It is constructive theological imagination that is able to see the potential significance of newly assessed biblical material and to enrich existing convictions on the basis of it; and it is the same constructive imagination that enables one to alter or modify existing convictions and build a structure that is better able to cope with the scriptural facts. Conversely, what we call "conservatism" in theology (and in this aspect it may be a "liberal," a "neoorthodox," a "moderate" or a "catholic" conservatism as well as a "conservative" one) is in large measure an inability to summon up the necessary theological imagination to accommodate any shift in position. People cannot imagine, cannot picture constructively, what an alternative position would be like; and therefore they refuse to contemplate the possibility. The fact is that many of the dogmatic positions found among students in exegesis are poorly related to the biblical material, so that very considerable imaginative effort is needed if their relationship to the latter is to be improved.

In putting the matter in this way, I have avoided the formulation, already mentioned, which has been so much used: Can exegesis be carried out, or even attempted, without theological presuppositions? This, though not unnatural, was a misguiding formulation. It was put as if the acknowledgment of these presuppositions was a great step forward which in itself led to some favorable results. This is not so. Of course most exegesis is done under theological presuppositions: but this fact is not an assurance of a good theological outcome. On the contrary, it is a recognition of the factor that is most likely to cause trouble and distortion of the biblical material. The theological fruitfulness of exegesis derives not from the existence of theological presuppositions but from the liveliness of the impact of the text upon these presuppositions. In fact many of those who joyously claim that there is no exegesis without theological presuppositions secretly twist this principle in a particular way: because one has certain presuppositions, they think, this gives an assurance that they can continue to adhere to these presuppositions and defend them against any pressures to change.

Conversely, the formulation in terms of theological presuppositions commonly proved too much. People were anxious to deny the supposed claims of critical scholarship to be "scientific" (although I know of little evidence that significant critical scholars made this claim) and to be free from theological presuppositions. Actually, there was never any doubt that the vast majority of critical scholarly operations were theologically driven and operated as part of theology. But, by making this a point of central principle, the common arguments pushed the matter too far, to the point where it came to seem to be claimed that no exegesis without theological presuppositions was possible at all. This might have made some sense so long as most exegetical study was done within institutions of a single tradition of theological learning, where all professors and students had a common heritage (say, Presbyterian, or Roman Catholic) of belief and style. Curiously, however, the argument about theological presuppositions became popular at just the time when its impossibility was coming to be most practically demonstrated through the increasing importance of departments of religion and the like, often in secular universities, in which biblical and other theological study was explicitly carried out in a mode that was independent of the personal faith of either teacher or student. The prevailing argument provided nothing for those who worked in such institutions: according to it, none of their activity could possibly take place. Documents of faith could not be understood except through the response of faith.

This just showed what should in any case long have been evident, namely that the argument in this form was impossibly solipsistic. To understand documents, even documents of a religion, one does not have to presuppose that these documents are true or valid, one does not have to be an adherent of that religion. Acceptance of the truth claims of texts is not an essential for the exegesis of them. If this were the case, no orthodox theologian could talk about Gnosticism, because he is not a Gnostic and regards that religion as thoroughly wrong. No Christian could say anything about Communism since only Marxists undertand it. No Christian could explain what Islam is all about or what ancient Semitic religion was like. We would all be walled up within the narrow compartments of that which we ourselves believe, unable either to explain or to understand any text other than that which was central to our own personal faith. Moreover, if the argument is pushed this far, there is no logical defence against the propagandist use of fact: indeed, the propagandist approach is the only one really open to us. No fair or dispassionate statements can be made, nor should one try to make them or expect them to be made.

All this is logically absurd and practically demonstrable as wrong. It is perfectly possible to make exegetical explanations separately from the question of the validity and truth of the viewpoints expressed in the texts. It may be difficult and require effort, but it is perfectly possible. What is needed is some adequate empathy and that same quantity, theological imagination, which has already been mentioned. For a Jew to understand a Christian document, or for a Christian to understand a Muslim document, requires the kind of theological imagination that can enter into what is going on in a faith that is not one's own. It may be difficult and require talent and experience but it is not in any way impossible. It may never be a-chieved in perfection but perfection is not needed: what is needed is adequacy. Description of religions, and exegesis of religious texts, that are not part of one's own belief, is a normal and viable part of religious discourse; and all theologians at least at some times take part in it. And, while some difficulty in understanding may come from one's distance from another religion, this is not in principle a greater difficulty than that which arises from the preconceptions engendered by a theology in relation to the texts upon which it itself relies.

But let us return to exegesis that is conducted amidst theologial assumptions and expectations, which is the normal type and was, contrary to common opinion, normal throughout the time of critical scholarship and until fairly recent times. The central question, as we have defined it, is how far biblical exegesis either (a) enriches the theological positions already held, and produces an alteration or modification of these positions or (b) fails to have any effect upon them. Now the material of the text does not have to be in itself directly "theological" in order to make an impact on theological conceptions. In marshalling the material of Scripture, exegesis takes note of evidences on many different levels. All of these are potentially "theological" because they have an effect on meaning and thereby on theological effect. But many of these elements of the text are of a nature over which theology as such cannot pronounce. Language questions are the most obvious example: the theological meaning of an Old Testament sentence may be affected by the constraints of the Hebrew verb tense system, but theology itself cannot say how that system works and the understanding of it depends on matters in linguistics that go far beyond the limits of the Bible or of biblical Hebrew. Similarly, text variants can have a drastic impact upon theological meaning. For instance, the textual uncertainty of several places where (according to some manuscripts) Christ is designated as "God" makes a tremendous difference, one way or the other, to the total impression made by the New Testament. Literary questions have a similar effect: the differential placing of the Cleansing of the Temple by Jesus (in John at the earliest stages of his ministry, in the Synoptics just before its end) immediately reflects upon the sort of literary works that one or more of the Gospels are, and thereby upon the total theological impact they are likely to have. Historical matters work in the same way: the question whether Quirinius can really have been governor of Syria at the time of a census which took place at the time of Jesus' birth (Luke 2:2) makes considerable difference to our idea of the sort of book that Luke is, and thereby again to the theological effect it is likely to have (recent study makes it highly unlikely that Quirinius could have been in that office at that time, that is, if Jesus was born during Herod's reign as in Matthew; the most natural explanation is that Luke just made a mistake and was confused by the later (and historically actual) census under Quirinius in 6 AD).[2] Observations from environing cultures and religions work in the same way: the law of the *herem*, commanding Israel to destroy all persons in captured Canaanite cities, along with all their animals, and to present their material possessions as an offering to the Lord, is immensely affected in theological scope and impact when we take into account the Moabite inscription describing how the Moabites did the same thing to Israel. Thus effects upon theological interpretation are exercised by facts, data, classifications and assessments that are not in themselves theological.

All this belongs, I believe, to the character of exegesis. In exegesis Scripture is set over against existing theological belief: not as an antagonist, indeed, but in the hope and expectation of fruitful interaction. Scripture itself is of course, as everyone now says, theological, and is there for theological (as also for liturgical and devotional) use. But the idea that Scripture is prime source and criterion for theology inevitably sets it somewhat on the other side, even if only temporarily and for the sake of sound and better theology. If one had remained with a more Catholic or Orthodox point of view, it might not have been so: Scripture and interpretative tradition would have melted sweetly into one another. But the very drastic isolation of Scripture as criterion in Protestantism has the unexpected and often scarcely detected effect of somewhat "secularizing" its mode of functioning. We do not see it as something harmonious with the contemporary theology or with the theology of the recent past: we ask it to give witness that will, if necessary, overthrow the concepts of recent, standard and customary theology and lead, where necessary, to reformation.

This "secularizing" effect does not come about because people cease to regard the Scripture as holy and inspired: on the contrary, it was the effect of insisting on biblical authority, of supposing that the text is to be the criterion for the theology that is to emerge. For this purpose the text has to be placed temporarily in a position where it stands over against our theological judgment. Biblical authority means that the text has to be theologically interpreted, but in such a way that the text criticizes and reforms the theological proposals that we place against it; and it does this by putting hard, concrete, and sometimes nontheological questions and pieces of evidence to the theological interpreter. Where are the words that say what you take to be the meaning? Why does one Gospel not mention such and such a matter, when another does? Where is the cultural evidence that might justify you in believing that this or that could have been the meaning?

This "secularizing" effect may seem strange: is not Scripture by its nature "holy"? Of course it is. But one of its main functions in relation to belief operates through its being a text, a body of written material with hard and knobby edges that make it awkward for faith. It seems to be canonization, especially when taken within the Protestant context, that has this effect. Unwritten tradition may perhaps fit in more smoothly and more subtly with that which is believed. Speakers, as they repeat it, modify it slightly, fitting it to the mood and the needs of the moment; they shape it subtly to fit what will be more acceptable. The Bible as a canonical text is a text: it does not adjust, it is still there as it was before, it does not make allowance for our frailties or our changes of fashion or tendency. Thus, in the exegetical process, given the two quantities, the pre-existing dogmatic convictions and expectations on the one side, and the text as it is on the other, the text stands there as an unmoving, unyielding, unsympathetic block of linguistic, textual and literary material, saying like Pilate: what I have written I have written (John 19.22). Of course, the total function of Scripture is a positive one: it nourishes faith, it builds theology, it supports obedience. Seen in the long term this is what it does. But it does this only because, and in the measure that, in the short term it stands like a heavy and intractable crag impeding the passage of the theologies with which we started out.

Thus theological exegesis is not something produced by an extension from nontheological exegesis, but is a dialectical relation between the text and theology. The issue of whether there are or are not theological presuppositions is really less important than it once seemed. My own teaching life in biblical studies has been roughly equally divided between teaching in theological institutions and teaching in departments of Hebrew, Semitic languages, religious studies and the like; and for the life of me I cannot see that there is any fundamental difference in exegetical method, logic or criteria of relevance between the one case and the other. The essential difference seems to be that in a theological context certain questions are likely to be asked which in the other context may be left unconsidered. But the mode in which evidence is brought from the text to bear upon these questions seems to be the same as when evidence is used in a nontheological context.

It is interesting, however, to consider what these questions are, the questions that are particularly typical of the theological context. They seem to me to resolve into two: the question of coherence and the question of truth. The question of coherence asks how far, and in what way, this text may be understood to form part of a coherent whole with other portions of the Bible, or with other texts that may be held to be basic sources for theology. Much of biblical theology has been concerned with this question. But even the question of coherence may be asked without a fully theological motive: works on biblical theology are perfectly acceptable as reading matter in departments of Hebrew or of religous studies. The question of how the thoughts of (say) the entire Hebrew Bible can be seen to hang together can be perfectly well asked without one's entering into theological commitment to these thoughts. In other words, the worlds of biblical theology and of history or description of ancient religion are a good deal closer than was once thought. But for theologians the question of coherence is mandatory, while for others it is in part optional.

The question of truth is more central. Theological exegesis is concerned with the questions: Is this true? or, In what sense is this true? It seems, however, that exegetical study on its own cannot give an answer to such questions. Even biblical theology on its own cannot do so, not in the more profound relations that may be relevant. That is to say, when exegesis reaches its more ultimate limits, it increasingly merges with the questioning and the thinking of systematic or dogmatic theology. The question "What is this text really saying?" cannot be answered, under these circumstances, without also answering the question "What is God really like?" which is an ultimate dogmatic question. To ask exegesis to extend itself to the point where it, alone, should answer such questions, is to demand of it something that it cannot perform.

But the handling of the question of truth in much modern exegesis was paradoxical. Barthian theology, in particular, tended to forbid the asking of the apologetic question, "Is this true?" According to it, theology began when the biblical witness was accepted, and there was no room for the questioning of its truth, nor was there any place to stand from which one might proceed with such a questioning. This tendency, contrary to its own intent, fitted in rather well with the feeling of exegetes that they could not handle questions of ultimate truth in any case. Some exegesis did indeed concern itself considerably with the historical-apologetic question, "Did this really happen?" and, "If not, what did happen?", but even then the influence of this line of questioning in modern exegesis is easily exaggerated: most commentaries, for instance, do not really attempt to tell us "what really happened" in the Exodus, the Transfiguration or the Resurrection. They tell us rather what the telling of these events mean for and in the biblical books being commented on. But much more did exegesis hold back from the discussing of the ultimate theological questions and the passing of judgments about them. Exegesis held back particularly from the dogmatic-apologetic question, "Is this picture of God really true?" But the avoidance of that question was the central reason why exegesis seemed to fail to "be theological." Those who most insisted that exegesis ought to "be theological" were also the ones who refused to it the means by which it could indeed link with theology. It is in the asking of the dogmatic-apologetic question, "Is this really true of God?" that exegesis most seriously impinges upon theology and is most seriously reacted upon by theology. If exegesis is to "be truly theological," it can only be so in so far as it engages with theology in the dialectical questioning about whether the biblical picture of God can be affirmed as true. We thus arrive at a position almost diametrically opposite to that which dominated much exegetical theory earlier in this century.

As we have seen, everything in the text and about the text has potential theological relevance. This has two complementary effects. Everything has potential theological effect, because everything has an effect upon meaning; but not everything is controllable by the discipline of theology itself. Theology in itself has no power to tell us what must be the correct text of a particular verse, or what are the semantic linkages between a group of Hebrew words, or why the Moabites slew all their Israelite captives. Theological exegesis is never and can never be a purely theological undertaking, in which only theological criteria matter. Theological results are the consequence of the impact upon the theological imagination of thousands of indications from the text and from around the text, many or most of which do not in themselves belong within the purview of theology itself. Theology, in so far as it is "biblical," must be built upon and depend upon material which it itself does not control.

On the other hand, the factuality of the text - the grammatical categories, the semantic linkages, the textual variants, the religious parallels - all this is not mere prolegomena, an assemblage of material that may perhaps later be theologically useful. To suppose so is the fault of that entire *instrumental* view, if we may so call it, of the exegetical process, the idea that these matters are "critical tools" which one has to learn to "use" but which are really only auxiliary or instrumental in their relation to real theological assessment. On the contrary: none of these things-grammatical forms and their categorial structure, semantic linkages and their implications, variant readings and the discipline of their evaluation, religious and cultural frameworks - none of these or of the disciplines that treat of them are "tools:" they are part of Scripture itself, they evidence the subtheological structure without which it would not have any meaning at all and would be uninterpretable. All of these are not instruments which must (perhaps painfully and regretfully) be learned up and thereafter used: they are part of the fabric of Scripture and part of its own means of conveying its own meaning to us.

This is significant, because an instrumental view of scholarly approaches to the Bible may well be influential among students, and especially so in the United States. We spoke earlier of the practical character of exegesis, but practicality does not mean that exegesis is a technique to be learned and followed out. An example of this is the linear conception of the exegetical process, depicted with a vivid awfulness by another Richmond professor, Sibley Towner, in his own inaugural lecture entitled "Holistic Exegesis."[3] As Towner delineates it, the "expository model in which we were all trained," which follows "the usual historical-critical way of doing things," required a strictly linear procedure. One had first to translate the text from Greek or Hebrew, taking note of the critical apparatus in case some variants should be found to be lurking there; then the literary operation of delimiting the pericope should be undertaken, so as to discern the flow of the argument. Then the historical and social background should be taken into account, and so also the source criticism and the like. Only after all this has been done, according to this model, can any statement be made about what the text meant. And only after that can one go on to consider what it might mean for modern believers who live in a different world.

Dr. Towner is right in seeing that I would reject such a linear model of the exegetical process. I differ only in that I do not think that any such linear model was ever characteristic of biblical criticism. Biblical criticism, in most of its forms, was much more theological than it appeared to be. We have to distinguish between the actual logic of biblical criticism and the way in which it was economic of space to present and display its operations. Thus it may well be convenient (I do not say that it must be so) to set out textual evidence and discussions first, then to proceed to literary analysis, to historical and social relevances, and so on, and only thereafter to proceed to a final theological evaluation. As an exercise for students, and as a typographical way to set out a commentary, this may gain in clarity and save cost and trouble. But the exegetical process does not actually work in this clear and simple linear sequence. To take the most obvious example, one cannot really translate the text from Hebrew or Greek, accurately and empathetically, until one has already considered the basic direction of the argument and the main theological thrust of the passage: and that means that the last element in the linear process must be thought out before the first step is seriously taken. In fact all these elements, distinguished in sequence in a linear model, are interlinked. This, however, was in my opinion already well known to the main stratum of critical scholarship. Only when critical scholarship was thought of as a technique or mechanical procedure to be followed out did these interrelations come to be thought of as an essentially linear sequence, which should be followed in order to ensure success. Something similar, incidentally, was the case with hermeneutics in general: people often thought of it as furnishing a practical guide how to do exegesis as if it set out a technical mode of operation which would lead to good theological results. The outcome of the fervent hermeneutical discussion of the mid-century should at least have shown that this is not the case.

This leads on, however, to another practical point of importance: the question of how commentaries can be written. Our argument has been: theological exegesis takes place as an interaction between the factuality of the text and the theological expectations that people have. Now it has often been said, as against the style of the modern commentary, that it provides an assembly of the factual data and relevant considerations but does not go on to specify the theological consequences that must follow. Put in the crudest terms, it does not tell you what, on the basis of the text studied, is to be believed. This fact has at times been lamented as a defect in commentaries; and some commentary series have sought to find a way to overcome this deficiency. But, on the basis of the account I have offered, one can see why this requisite, namely, the statement of the theological consequences, is not easily to be provided within the framework of a commentary on a biblical book. For the theological consequences do not follow directly from the facts of the biblical book alone, but from the interaction of these facts with other texts and with the pre-existing theological assumptions and expectations of the reader. But these assumptions and expectations are highly variable, and in any case cannot be clearly predicted by the writer of the commentary. In earlier times, when a commentary was essentially written for an audience denominationally defined, this may have been different. One might write, let us say, for a Presbyterian or for a Roman Catholic readership; the previous theological assumptions might be reasonably well knowable; and one might have a set of positive theological next steps to suggest to such an audience. But this is no longer the case. In order to map out the theological futures that would follow from a biblical book, one would have to write different series of commentaries — one, let us say, for Bultmannians tinged with liberation theology, another for conservatives attracted to structuralism, yet another for moderate Anglicans well integrated with society culture, and so on. For this reason it is quite difficult to write commentaries that will actually tell the reader whether women should be ordained, what should be done about nuclear weapons or about the situation in South Africa, and so on. In other words, the apparent reluctance of the commentary to address directly the theological and ethical questions of the present day is not necessarily a fault; nor is it a consequence of a "historical" orientation that refuses to face modern problems. It is, on the contrary, a decision perfectly seriously grounded in theological principle, in the fact that theological consequence does not follow directly from the text itself but only from its interaction with other texts and with pre-existing theological tradition. Since the nature of that tradition is highly variable, it is a perfectly responsible theological decision that the commentary cannot handle all the possibilities of theological consequence but must concentrate on providing and discussing the evidence of the text itself, within its own environment, the impact of which evidence upon the theological assumptions forms the core of theological exegesis. When this is not done, the commentary can become in certain aspects a tendentious plea for some point of view, theological or nontheological, conservative or anticonservative, denominational or culture-bound. This should not be surprising. After all, of all the commentaries written, a large proportion are not written in order to promote fresh theological thinking but in order to prevent it, that is, to support and safeguard entrenched positions and to discourage people from leaving them.

To sum up, then, theological exegesis was never really in danger or in doubt: the main body of exegetical work was always theologically motivated and looked toward theological ends. It served these theological ends, however, not so much by making explicit the theological consequences, and more by assembling, evaluating and presenting the textual material that was (or might be) relevant for these theological conclusions. In doing this it was - even if rather unconsciously - recognizing the reality of the exegetical situation and responding suitably to its actual needs.

What has been said above may seem to be a reasonable account, well based in common sense and in the actuality of what happens in exegetical practice. If so, why should it appear strange? The answer is certainly: because it differs from some of the major popular trends in hermeneutical theory that have been influential in the last few decades. This brings us back to James Mays' inaugural lecture. He was right to mention in it the fate of the Quest of the historical Jesus: for in all exegetical discussion there was no influence that in those days hung over us more threateningly than the fate of that Quest. It was the prime example that overshadowed us all, its story was the warning that was set over the entrance to the exegetical Hades. Although Mays and I were primarily Old Testament scholars, the shadow of the historical Jesus brooded over that discipline just as much as over New Testament studies, indeed possibly even more. New Testament scholars, we may suspect, learned to take the Jesus of history more equably as a problem; for some trends in Old Testament study it stayed on as a traditional bogy, a scarecrow to frighten those who might wish to walk in unfamiliar paths. As Mays then said, the "Old Quest" was deemed to have been a failure; there were rumours of a "New Quest" which would work on different principles, but one could not be sure if anything would come of it. In any case Mays did not profess to have produced any clear picture of the Jesus of history, nor did I; and that question we shall leave aside. What is important, and what we realized very clearly, was the lessons that were then customarily drawn from the fate of the Quest; and these lessons were believed to have very clear and striking implications for the theory and practice of exegesis. It was, I suggest, the assessment of the Quest that dominated much exegetical theory, even in the Old Testament area (and perhaps more in it than in the New Testament area), and especially in the English-speaking world, most of all in the United States. The fate of the Quest, and the hermeneutical and theological directions that were taken in order to avoid a repetition of that fate, were extremely influential in all our thinking about exegesis.

If the Quest was such a failure, why has it never really gone away? Why are people still interested in something that is understood to have been so complete a failure? Why can they not simply accept that there is no access except to the Christ of faith, no means of getting behind the documents to a "historical" reality?

After all, if the Quest was such a failure, it is remarkable how much work has been done by serious scholars that seemed to continue it in some form. An impressive book was written by H. Bornkamm. Important articles were written by Käsemann, Ebeling and Fuchs, all highly respected scholars and theologians; and J.M. Robinson sought to direct the impact of their work towards the United States in the form of the "New Quest." Other important articles were written by Dahl, by Conzelmann, by O. Michel, by H. Bartsch. A significant book was published in America in 1971 by Leander Keck.[4] None of these seemed content to let the question of the historical Jesus simply disappear into the past as if it were a false turning taken by older scholarship. There was, they seemed to say, something in the question that was exegetically and theologically valid and that could not be allowed to escape without an impoverishment of Christian faith. In an inaugural lecture at Princeton Theological Seminary in 1985, James H. Charlesworth put it so:

> What do I consider the central task of the New Testament scholar? It is to seek what can be known about the life and teachings of Jesus of Nazareth. This contention should shake loose many shelved conclusions regarding methods and sources.[5]

Some British scholarship emphasized the question even more strongly. Of C.H. Dodd George Caird wrote:

Precisely because he believed in a God who was Lord of history and who had revealed himself in a human life, he was committed to the quest of the historical Jesus by all the rigours of academic discipline.[6]

And Caird himself, a scholar of central Reformed tradition, and deeply theological in his central perceptions, spoke even more strongly:

Anyone who believes in the Incarnation, whether he be Catholic or Protestant, and whether he likes it or not, is committed to the quest of the historical Jesus.[7]

Now undoubtedly in saying this Caird was saying something different from the ideas that had motivated the old Quest for the Jesus of history, and no doubt something very different also from the ideas of the new Quest.[8] But it was still a quest that he was insisting upon, and a quest for the historical Jesus. Here, from within an emphatic belief in the Incarnation, and in strong opposition to any skepticism in the approach to the Bible (Caird emphatically opposed the skepticism, as he saw it, of the Bultmannian approach), was a strong insistence upon the historical Jesus as a theological necessity! This may not count as typical; but it is a symptom of something that has remained widespread: the question of the historical Jesus continues to have an active place on the theological agenda. For a long time we had the impression that the fate of the old Quest had shown that practically nothing relevant for faith could be gained from the historical Jesus and that we can have no access at all except to the apostolic witness to the Christ of faith. The reverse seems now to be the case: all that argumentation that affected us so powerfully seems now to be ignored, and the majority opinion seems to be that knowledge of the historical Jesus is of vital importance for religious faith.

For this there are some rather obvious reasons. For one thing, the lessons drawn by many theologians from the outcome of the original Quest were all too convenient and comfortable for the church. There is, we were repeatedly told, no access to any information that might tell us anything about Jesus as he lived and thought that differs in substance from the authoritative biblical witness. "Oh yeah?" say people in their vulgar way. Cultural judgments have gone in the opposite direction: if people are interested in Jesus, they are likely to think that a nonbeliever will ask the questions and face the facts more honestly than someone who speaks for the church's tradition. And, as Käsemann remarked, the output of novelistic portrayals of Jesus testifies to a deep need to know something of Jesus as a credible human person.

The rise of departments of religion, as distinct from faculties of theology, already mentioned above, makes a similar point in another way. Religion may be validly studied as an academic subject by persons who are adherents of other religious traditions from the one they are studying, or of no religious tradition at all. If the conclusion so often presented as the consequence of the Quest is right and if one has no access to Jesus except through acceptance in faith of the apostolic proclamation of the risen Christ, then really nothing can be said about Jesus within a department of this kind. In fact it is obvious that some kind of valid discussion of Jesus and his life and teaching can be carried on and is carried on within such institutions. But this fact proves that there was something wrong with a theory that maintained that such a kind of study of Jesus was simply impossible. It is ironic that the view of the uselessness and impossibility of any knowledge of the historical Jesus came to its highest point of acceptance at just about the same time when educational experience proved that it could not be right.

These considerations have been all the more reinforced in the postwar period by the rising importance of Jewish scholarship, in the New Testament area just as much as in that of the Old. Jewish scholars, often of great learning, write about Jesus. Not only so, but wide trends within Christianity welcome it. In the older discussion about the Quest this was hardly taken into account.[9] It was very much a problem within Christendom, a conflict between an older Christianity that built upon traditional doctrinal formulations and newer Christianity that built upon the historical Jesus. What Jews might think was then a secondary and marginal matter. Today this is no longer the case. Jewish study of the question is highly regarded and is esteemed from the Christian side as a very positive contribution. But there is no way for Jews to study Jesus or to say anything about him at all except on a historical basis. Jews cannot begin by presupposing the truth of the apostolic kerygma: they have to start and to work on the basis of the historical Jesus. Thus a substantial piece of study like Geza Vermes' Riddell Lectures has a considerable typological similarity to the older Quest in spite of great differences in content.[10] The common theological arguments that there is no real access to the historical Jesus have simply got to be rejected by Jewish investigators. It is ironic, therefore, that many of the Christian scholars who emphasize the value of the common heritage with

Judaism and who insist upon the embedding of Jesus in Jewish culture are also people who continue to oppose any positive interest in the historical Jesus: for these two viewpoints are surely contradictory. It is not possible to accept that the study of Jesus and of Christian origins is a common field for Jewish and Christian scholarship, and at the same time to insist that the study of the historical Jesus is not a productive avenue.

This essay will not argue a case about the historical Jesus for itself, but will concentrate on the lessons which were drawn from the matter and which were supposed to provide interpretative guidelines for future exegesis.

1. The first point, and one repeatedly made, was the argument from difficulty: historical reconstruction is extremely difficult because of the small amount of the material and its complicated and ambiguous character. It will be very hard to discover what the Jesus of history was like, and there is no hope of achieving agreement in such matters. The attempt should therefore not be made.

The argument from difficulty is a serious one, and even if every other consideration was in favour of the Quest this might prove that it could not succeed, in the sense that it could not lead to an agreed, recognized and credible picture of the historical Jesus. But this is not an objection in principle, or, as Perrin puts it, it is not a "methodological" objection.[11] It means only that paucity and ambiguity of the material make reconstruction too difficult.

This however does not settle the matter, and indeed this argument can easily be turned round in the opposite direction. Firstly, it is likely that many of those who are so deeply conscious of the great practical difficulties of the Quest are so because they do not want any such Quest to be attempted at all. Secondly, it is a mistake to regard the older Quest, as is often done, as an example of the "historical" approach in contrast with the "theological." The reverse seems to be true. The Quest was theological in character throughout: the "historical" Jesus was sought precisely because it was believed that the historical Jesus would be theologically paramount. Thus the Quest did not typify the work of "historical criticism"; on the contrary, it was historical criticism that destroyed the older Quest.[12] The older Quest belonged to the realm of speculative theology, rather than to that of historical criticism. Thus the failure of the older Quest, seen in this way, was not because historical study could not cope with the life of Jesus, but because speculative theology offered too many varieties of possible constructions.

Thirdly, it could be argued that the principle of the historical

Jesus is not in any case dependent on the achievement of success in reconstructing what he was like. Once the point is made that Jesus in his life, teaching and intentions was not congruent in every aspect with all the material of the Gospels and with all traditional Christology, then it may be that the essential point has been made: in this sense, contrary to all that is said, the old Quest may be deemed to have been successful. Jesus, as seen on the basis of the evidence of the Gospels, was in some very important mode different from the Christ of post-Easter faith and of later Christology - and surely this is generally admitted.

Fourthly, the argument from difficulty may lead in a different direction from that which is expected. Extreme difficulty of this kind may be a quite normal feature of all investigation of the founders of religions. Jesus is not at all unique in this, nor even an extreme case. Zoroaster, for instance, presents a much more unique degree of uncertainty. At least we agree about the century in which Jesus lived; experts on Zoroaster may date him as late as 400 BC or as early as 1500 BC or before.[13] It may be just a characteristic of founders of religions that traditions and interpretations of their lives and teaching grow so fast, become so controlling, and govern the presentation of the original material so completely, that penetration back into the actual life of the founder becomes practically impossible. But this, if right, does not point toward the absolute uniqueness of Jesus but towards a special and unusual but by no means exceptional category in terms of the history of religions. The difficulty of reconstructing the historical Jesus does not therefore necessarily point towards a theological solution in terms of acceptance of the church's kerygma and later Christology.

Thus the difficulty of historical reconstruction is not a valid argument against our recognizing the importance of the historical Jesus.

2. The second argument is that the New Testament documents are of a confessional and committed religious character and are not written as objective accounts of historical information. Because they are kerygmatic and confessional in character, they cannot rightly be used as sources from which historical information may be extracted. Surely this is mere nonsense, and it is surprising that anyone was ever taken in by so obviously wrong an argument. The fact that documents are confessional, or indeed that they are of any other character whatever, is no reason at all why they cannot be used as evidence for historical study. History is not something that can be derived only from sources that are themselves already pure

history or objective fact. History is written on the basis of sources such as newspapers, speeches of politicians, opinions of ill-informed witnesses, time-serving poetry, self-exonerating memoirs of military leaders, and - not least - propaganda. None of these are objective factual reporting and all are in their way "confessional" or "kerygmatic" documents: but good history works from them all and all historians are accustomed to using them. The fact that documents are kerygmatic is just no reason why historical conclusions should not be extracted from them or based upon them.

In any case there is another qualification that should be added. The fact that documents as a whole are intended to be confessional does not mean that every sentence and phrase within them has that character. Even within the most confessional documents certain elements, smaller or larger, were there not because of confessional reasons but because they provided historical locations and indications relevant to the story. St Luke's mention of Quirinius as governor of Syria, whether accurate or not, was surely not put there as a "kerygmatic" element, but because Luke thought of it as a date or historical location. Thus what is true of a biblical book as a whole need not be true of all its parts. The confessional nature of books like the Gospels is just no reason why usable historical data should not be found in them. Doubtless the argument had some valid basis if it was applied to the older Quest, in which some had the idea that there existed some source or body of material that was entirely historical and free from the distortions caused by theology. But as a general argument about the usability of biblical evidence for historical study it is entirely wrong. Moreover, I have understated rather than overstated the degree to which the Gospels furnish data and depictions that are in style appreciably different from the style of the post-Easter kerygma. "It is now obvious to the leading New Testament scholars that pre-Easter data are preserved in the Gospels," says Charlesworth.[14]

3. More serious is the argument that it is theologically wrong to seek for any historical reality behind the Scriptures. According to this view one simply cannot go behind the apostolic witness. There is for Christian faith no Jesus other than the Christ of faith. "The Jesus of the Christian church - the Christ of faith - is only known by means of the authoritative witness of his disciples."[15] This is the approach that has been so widely and repeatedly pressed upon us as authoritative since theology reacted to the fate of the older Quest.

But a little thought quickly reveals its untenability as a principle of Christian faith. For it leaves open the possibility that the Jesus attested by the apostolic witness never existed in that shape or character. There may never have been any Jesus who was like the person portrayed in that witness. Or there may have been a Jesus, but he was a person whose life, ideas, teaching and theology were quite unlike those of the apostolic presentation of him. Taking it in this way, the church must believe the apostolic witness but "believing" is here used in an unusual way, for one must "believe" the witness but in such a way that one cannot and must not affirm that things were actually so. The apostolic witness may then misrepresent what Jesus was: the Christ of faith may then be the authoritative interpretation of Jesus but that does not prevent it being an erroneous interpretation of him. This is, as I understand it, the question expressed by writers like Käsemann and Ebeling as the question of "continuity." Can we affirm that the apostolic witness has real continuity with that which it interprets, with the life, teaching and purposes of one who actually lived, and if so in what kind of continuity? There seem to be three possibilities here:

a. One may stick to principle and insist that one cannot at all go behind the apostolic witness, so that absolutely no appeal can be made to any "historical" reality of Jesus that is theologically relevant.

b. One may affirm that the historical Jesus can in fact be known and in fact more or less congruent with the way in which the apostolic witness depicted him. This is the traditional conservative-historical argument. It completely contradicts position (a) but is in fact often combined with (a). In that case (a) is overtly maintained but it is secretly implied throughout that the historical identity of Jesus was as required by position (b).

c. One may affirm that something can be known of the historical Jesus that differs from the post-Easter witness to him, and maintain that the degree and mode of continuity between the two is a main form of theological elucidation of him.

Position (a) in its more drastic forms is a very extreme argument, so much so that it is hard to believe that anyone really accepts it. Those who do generally smuggle back in the conservative-historical argument (b) in order to provide their Christ with some kind of human identity. Or else they adopt a total framework of Christianity such that the pivot lies elsewhere and the relation between Jesus as he lived and Jesus as proclaimed in the kerygma is just not very important. But, extreme as position (a) may be, and repugnant to the sense of most Christian traditions, it is the one which has been very influential on the development of hermeneutical theories and proposals. Position (a) may perhaps be regarded as a failure of theological imagination. The question of a historical Jesus, different in some respect from the Christ of the apostolic witness, causes such fears that it must be completely abolished; no attempt is to be made to accommodate the concept of the Jesus of history within theology. Rather than permit this, severe breaches with theological tradition in other respects are to be made. For it can hardly be doubted that, of the three positions described above, it is (b), the conservative-historical one, that has the extensive rootage in Christian tradition. The high regard and veneration for the dominical words, the actual sayings of Jesus, along with his acts, is deeply embedded in both Catholic and Protestant faith and piety. The Quest for the historical Jesus, in emphasizing the historical sayings as it did, was continuing along the lines of this ancient tradition. It was position (a) that was the innovation as against classical theology: the idea that nothing much could be known about the historical Jesus, and that it was wrong to attach importance to the question, was a greater breach with the older Christianity. And, finally, position (a) left open the horrid possibility, repugnant to most of those who held it, that the apostolic witness, being unconnectable with historical realities that lay behind it, was in the end a myth.[16]

4. Another objection is to the "downgrading" of that which is classified as less "historical." There is reason in this objection because just such a judgment was common in the older Quest and continues to be found in scholarship. Many people now dislike the idea that one should ascribe a high rank to that which is deemed historical and a lower rank to that which is less so. I here leave aside the question whether people are right in this or wrong. My point is another one: namely, that no such value judgment is necessarily involved in the concept of the historical Jesus. The question can be put in quite other terms: in terms of before and after. What was there in the life, action, teaching and theology of Jesus, before his death and within the interpretative matrix of his life and ministry, that led up to and brought about the events of his Passion? And in what ways are these different from the same as seen from the perspective after the Resurrection and as interpreted in the post-Easter apostolic witness? In neither case are we seeking "pure" and objective historical facts, separated from interpretation; we are talking about two distinguishable stages of theologically interpreted tradition. It would thus be perfectly possible, at least in theory, to

distinguish certain elements or patterns as belonging to the historical Jesus and understood or intended by him in a certain way, while remaining convinced that other and newer interpretations later attached actually expressed the theological realities better. Thus the question of distinguishing between the historical Jesus and later interpretations is in principle a quite different one from the question of discovering something that, because it has historical character, has higher authority. The reasonings and intentions with which Jesus lived and went to his death may be ultimately less final and less authoritative than the meanings which the church, in the light of the Resurrection, saw in these events: conceivably so, at any rate. But the meanings and interpretations perceived by the church lose considerably in significance if they cannot at all be put in relation with the pre-Easter Jesus.

5. The same is true of the objection that the idea of the historical Jesus entails the stripping away of theology in order to discover an original nontheological Jesus. As a memory of the older Quest, this view may be well justified; but it has no logical necessity about it. The idea of an interest in the historical Jesus is not necessarily to discover a nontheological Jesus but may be to discover a Jesus whose theological position was different in time, in situation and in structure. In this view the historical Jesus is important precisely because he is a theological Jesus and an authoritative theological Jesus. It was the theology of the historical Jesus, within his own framework of meaning within Judaism, that acted to bring about his rejection and death and thereby the salvation of mankind. For Christianity, there must have been some vital continuity between this theology and the theology by which the church later proclaimed him as the Christ. But such a continuity does not mean an identity; on the contrary, it is meaningful only where there is also a difference. That difference may be a very essential part of the understanding of Jesus. Thus it is a red herring when we suppose that the concept of the historical Jesus entails the stripping away of theology in order to produce a nontheological Jesus.

6. The most vivid, however, of the negative impressions left by the Quest of the historical Jesus was the idea that the questers found a Jesus who was an image of themselves and of their own theological concerns. As Tyrrell said of Harnack, it was like a man looking down a deep well, who saw at the bottom only the reflection of a liberal Protestant face looking up.[17] True enough; and yet not the whole truth. As Donald Baillie already saw, the same argument

could be used in other directions: Bultmann's Jesus, he suggested, was but the reflection of a Barthian face looking up.[18]

It was true, indeed, that the older Quest found its own face at the bottom of the well. Looking back on it, however, one must feel that the more orthodox brethren, who were after all much the majority, used this argument in an unfair and even somewhat unscrupulous way. If it was true that the old Questers saw themselves reflected at the bottom of the well, the same could perhaps have been said of those who rejected the Quest. Roman Catholics saw a papal face at the bottom of the well, others saw the face of the traditional Christology, which for them was their own face; conservative evangelicals certainly saw a conservative evangelical face. In other words, if the gibe about the reflected face was valid, it was not really a proper criticism of the Quest for the historical Jesus: it could be fairly and properly used only if one said that *all* Christian currents saw their own image at the bottom of the well. This, no doubt, had always been so; but the Quest had done it in a different way.

At the end of the older Quest, however, there was a significant shift - the introduction of what we may call the "negative-image" Jesus. This comes in with Johannes Weiss and Schweitzer. The jest about the face at the bottom of the well implies crudity: it was very crude of the old Quest to make its Jesus into someone very like its own supporters. It was less crude, and more sophisticated, to say that the historical Jesus was quite different from what one oneself was, indeed pretty well the opposite. The historical Jesus of Weiss and Schweitzer was an apocalyptic fanatic, quite unlike their own modern Ritschlian and bourgeois selves. This approach is less crude, but in principle it is just as easy, there is nothing in it; and the result is just as satisfactory. Jesus is not like the modern theologian, but he is like what the modern theologian has room in his system for him to be.

From this it was a short step to the "blank-image" face of Jesus. Jesus is there all right, he's down the well, you can tell that it is he, but his face has no shape, no contours; all you can tell is that it is a human face of some kind. Some currents of the dialectical theology followed this direction. Jesus was a human person - that was essential. He must have had some opinions and done some teaching, but it is of no theological value to enquire what these opinions were and it would not make any difference if we did know. Such an approach appeared to offer some theological gains. It meant that no salvation was to be found through following the teachings of the historical

Jesus, a theme associated with liberal theology. Salvation lay outside man, outside the human realm; it lay not in what Jesus taught, but in what God had done through him. Jesus was more a conductor of salvation than a teacher of it or (even worse) an example of how to attain it. But this had its paradoxical aspects. In a time when "theology" was being revived and becoming more and more the essential thing, and when it was being more and more urged that everything in the Bible was theological, Jesus became practically the only exception: he alone had no theology worth knowing about.

A really strong-minded devotee of the blank-face approach, therefore, might have accepted that Jesus and his ideas were very contrary to his own. A really convinced Barthian should have been able to admit that the historical Jesus may have been a Philonic adherent of Greek philosophy and an upholder of natural theology. Admittedly there is little evidence that this was so, but we have no right to examine the question on the basis of evidence at all. Even if Jesus held these views, this fact would not make any difference to Christian theology, which is hostile to Greek philosophy and denies natural theology. Similarly, Jesus might in real life have been a Zealot or Jewish nationalist, but for Chritianity this would not matter, and the Christ of the church would be as depicted in the Gospels, where most of this nationalism has been stripped away, leaving only small traces behind.

But on the whole such strong-minded adherents of the "blank-face" approach are few. Most people, including scholars and theologians, want a Jesus they can approve of in some way, within their own set of theological values. Few would be willing to rest content with a Jesus who in historical fact was an unprincipled crook, a used-chariot salesman of the time, a dishonest and self-seeking politician. Though it suited some kinds of theological position to have a blank face for the historical Jesus, few or none have been able to accept and maintain that view consistently. This brings us back to the underlying question: belief in the Christ of the apostolic witness must necessarily imply some adequate continuity with what he did, and thought, and said, and was, in his earthly ministry. If it was only in the light of the Resurrection that all these were made significant, it was also only in the light of what Jesus had been beforehand that the Resurrection itself was made significant: the resurrecting of just anyone would not have signified the salvation of mankind. It was the Resurrection of the Jesus who had been what he had historically been that bore ultimate theological meaning.

Thus the "blank-face" approach, which was influential under the dialectical theology, was just as much a reflection of the theologian's own needs and ideals at the bottom of the well, as was the liberal face of Jesus under the older Quest. In Barthianism, in particular, the answer given to the question of the historical Jesus fitted in exactly with one of the major imperatives of that theology, namely, that there should be no apologetic discussion whatever in theology. This issue alone was sufficient, perhaps, to determine the position taken about the Jesus of history.

To sum up this point, then, the idea that the old Quest simply saw its own face reflected is in itself no serious objection to the quest of a historical Jesus; contrary, and later, theologies did the same thing but in a more sophisticated, dialectical and ironic way. In either case the image of Jesus was cast to suit the needs of a modern (even if conservative) theology.

As has been suggested, it was difficult for many to maintain the "blank face" image of Jesus in the long run. The later scholars in the Bultmannian tradition returned to a positive interest in the Jesus of history. Some Barthians, aware of the danger that the apostolic witness would turn out to be a myth, took the same direction.[19] But it may be that the main Barthian tradition reverted in considerable measure to the historical-conservative position: the historical Jesus was essential, but he was, as it happens, identical with the apostolic presentation of him.[20] This was not unnatural: but it was also a negation of the basic position on the historical Jesus that had been central to the dialectical theology from the start. It also denied that part of Martin Kähler's argument which had been its strongest element; namely, its refusal to go along the historical-conservative route.[21] It marked that rapprochement between Barthianism and Protestant conservative biblicism which has been noticeable in certain circles of English-speaking theology in the last decades.

It cannot be said, then, that the matter of the historical Jesus was a good proving ground for ideas of biblical interpretation. Whatever view we hold of the importance of the historical Jesus, the attempt to draw lessons from the quest for him and to apply them to biblical hermeneutics was badly handled. Martin Kähler's influential book, in English *The So-called Historical Jesus and the Historic Biblical Christ*, [22] is a good example. It is perhaps the most important single work to be strongly against the Jesus of history and to espouse the view that nothing relevant to Christian faith can be gained by going behind the testimony as we have it in the Bible. Kähler must have been a great man, as is seen from the influence he exercised upon Barth, Bultmann and Tillich. Yet the book seems to be largely wrong in its argumentation, and this for two reaons: firstly, the author simply did not take into account all the possibilities and insisted on framing the question in terms of only two or three types of situation; secondly, the whole argument is predicated entirely upon one particular type of Christianity, his own, and does not consider how the question might work from within a different total structure of theology. This is symptomatic. Some of the ideas that have been most powerful in their influence upon biblical interpretation were never worked out on the basis of what happened in practical interpretative work: they were really arguments for a particular theological position. Nowhere was this more the case than with arguments about the Jesus of history. People writing about this problem were often primarily motivated by the drive to find a satisfactory position for the question of the historical Jesus within their own theological system; and their interpretative remarks were often harnessed to this task. It is not surprising that discussions that are still dominated by the question of the historical Jesus are confusing, extreme, and often destructive when they are allowed to assume centrality in our hermeneutical principles.

The "New Quest" of the historical Jesus, introduced as such to the American theological public by James M. Robinson, was doubtless a much more sophisticated affair than the old one. As a discussion which affected ideas about interpretation, however, it very possibly had even more damaging effects. The New Quest - at least in its American form - seems not to be primarily directed toward finding out something about Jesus. Its purpose - though not necessarily that of its learned German originators whom it professes to follow - seems often to be not so much to find out anything about Jesus, but rather to introduce a new overarching conceptuality into American theology. The actual hermeneutical suggestions seem to be subordinate to the primary goal of introducing and explaining this general conceptual pattern, which, it was suggested, would impart a new dynamics and progress to American thinking.

But it is just this conceptuality that is the major problem about the New Quest, as about the "New Hermeneutic" which was associated with it.[23] The validity of this conceptual scheme is largely just assumed by Robinson; conversely, if one does not share this conceptuality, much of what is said about the New Quest is not so much wrong but largely meaningless. The entire operation is conceived and openly expressed as an importation of a major German conceptual pattern into America. It is significant that Robinson in a long footnote on his first two pages more or less contemptuously dismisses most ongoing French, British and American work on the subject, classifying it as merely a continuation of the original Quest.[24] This is not because he necessarily ignores the scholarly contributions there made, but because basically his case has no room for any conceptuality other than the particular German one that he presents. Moreover, by doing it in this way he is led to emphasize the German philosophical background upon which he depends much more than do the German scholars whom he is actually following, who seem in proportion to be more interested in the historical Jesus and less in Dilthey, Heidegger and Gadamer.

There are two obvious problems about this. Firstly, twentieth-century theology, especially through Barth's influence, has been acutely conscious of the danger involved if some particular philosophy is accepted as basic or even authoritative as the framework for theology. Why should all these very justified warnings be so blithely ignored? Moreover, in this respect Barth was followed by many exegetical scholars who were far from being Barthians in theology. The general trend throughout modern exegesis has been opposed to the mingling of philosophy with exegetical work. Why should that caution now be thrust aside?

But, secondly, if we are to have a philosophy, should we not make sure that it is a true philosophy? Do we not need to subject it to a searching philosophical critique, before we declare it valid as a basis for exegetical and theological work? The outstanding and remarkable feature of the proposal for a New Quest is that the philosophical framework imposed is accepted entirely uncritically, without any attempt whatever to ask "Is this true or valid?" And this is not the case with Robinson alone, but with other theology scholars who have attempted to build a hermeneutic for theology upon this philosophical tradition: Thiselton's *The Two Horizons* [25] is another clear example. If one favors this philosophical tradition, it seems that no more is felt necessary than to quote the great men, to elucidate their often difficult vocabulary, and to expound their thought. To ask, critically, whether it is true or valid, seems to be taken as unnecessary!

All this might not have mattered much if there had been universal professional acceptance that the Heidegger tradition of philosophy was basically right and the best that the world-wide culture could offer. But this is not at all the case. On the contrary, the Oxford philosophical tradition accords only a very low value to Heidegger's thinking and on the whole refuses to take it seriously as philosophy at all, regarding it as something closer to the category of poetry or imaginative literature. Naturally, such judgments are not necessarily true: Oxford philosophers may be stupid, insular, prejudiced and the like, as they are quite often told they are; it is also possible that time might bring a higher degree of recognition of the Heidegger type of thinking by British philosphy. But it is almost incredible that a current of biblical hermeneutics should strive to impose as its regulative philosophy a manner of thinking that is clearly rejected by the main philosophical stream of the English-speaking peoples at the present time, and all this without even asking the question or subjecting the philosophy in question to a critical enquiry.

In respect of biblical exegesis, however, the New Quest brought a further series of problems. Heidegger's thought was antipositivist and antiobjectivist. Robinson's way of justifying the New Quest, which was supposed to follow this philosophical approach, was to characterize the older Quest as positivist and objectivizing in its methods. The old, nineteenth-century historiography had been of this nature; modern historiography, following Dilthey, Heidegger, Collingwood and others, was concerned with history as "the act of intention, the commitment, the meaning for the participants, behind the external occurrence."[26] This, we hear, is important for "the modern concept of selfhood," and this in turn is relevant for the Jesus of history.[27] Since the old Quest was taken as a prime example of what historical criticism was like, it followed that classical biblical scholarship had been positivistic and objectivizing.

Thus the mode by which the New Quest was justified had the effect of seriously misrepresenting nineteenth-century historical work, twentieth-century historical work, and biblical criticism of all periods. None of these were correctly represented in the literature about the New Quest. "Nineteenth-century historiography and biography were modelled after the natural sciences," Robinson writes.[28] Only with post-Dilthey "modern" historiography does one begin to think about acts of intention, about meaning for the participants. The nineteenth century "saw the reality of the historical facts' as consisting largely in names, places, dates, occurrences, sequences, causes, effects - things which fall far short of being the actuality of history, if one understands by history the distinctively human, creative, unique, purposeful, which distinguishes man from nature."[29] All this was vastly exaggerated and the general impression it created was quite wrong. Most nineteenth-century history writing was not positivist in this sense or in any meaningful sense. To a large extent its fault was the opposite, namely, that it was often highly ideological and unduly motivated by philosophical ideals. To some extent the interpretation of the older history writing as positivistic was an American creation, as I myself argued twenty years ago.[30] Ranke's famous phrase, that history should be told *wie es eigentlich gewesen*, was widely interpreted in American tradition as a positivist ideal, because of the centrality of ideals of natural science in the United States. But Ranke did not mean this at all: on the contrary, his history from time to time invokes historical purpose and even divine intention, exactly the opposite of that which has been attributed to him.

Equally mistaken is it to suppose that modern history writing can be airily indifferent to the actuality of events. To dismiss positivism as if there was no element in historical work that rightly has a somewhat positivist character is extremely misleading. To say that there are no facts without interpretation is a comforting half-truth; it remains perfectly possible, even if difficult, to distinguish between factual and nonfactual, and the distinction is essential for the task of weighing and evaluating what purport to be interpretations. This has to go on in modern historical work just as much as in that of any previous period. Moreover, for the question of the historical Jesus this is particularly important. One has the impression of the impact of the New Quest that, if it has achieved anything in American scholarship, this has lain in areas like the meaning of parables, which may have been suitably enlarged through its ideas of language; but, apart from that, in matters of what Jesus did or did not do it has achieved rather little. For this its own presentation of modern historiographical method may well be responsible.

Nor, in particular, was biblical criticism "positivistic" in its approach. To me it seems incredible that such a picture should have been disseminated by anyone who knew what the biblical scholars of the critical tradition, at least in the English-speaking lands, were like. They were for the most part pious theologically-minded men, for whom the authority of the Bible was paramount. Their training was almost entirely in the older humanities: indeed, in a very large percentage, in the Latin and Greek classics along with some philosophy. They knew little of modern science and were distrustful of its ethos though not rejecting its results. They were not in the slightest inclined to take the natural sciences as the model for their theory of knowledge. A position like that of Collingwood, which is taken by Robinson to typify the "modern" approach as against the older, is just what most of them would have welcomed. It was human ideas, not natural facts, that were central. Events were meaningful because of grand concatenations of intentions and purposes. This idealist view of history fitted in, as most of them saw it, with their own theological concerns.

There was one other and particular aspect in which the heritage of Heidegger impinged unfortunately upon exegesis: his use of language, and in particular his etymological adventures. In my own work on semantics I paid little attention to Heidegger because he was not directly concerned in biblical scholarship. But it is not to be doubted that Heidegger is the richest source of absurd etymological fancies to be found anywhere in contact with theology in modern times. These have sometimes been excused on the grounds that the history of words must have had an effect upon their later meaning. But of course the etymologies that Heidegger offers and uses do not belong to the history of words at all. They are not histories, but inventions, fancies conjured up out of the author's own philosophy. And indeed Heidegger himself probably knew this quite well: these were for him illustrations through which language illustrated or expressed something that, according to him, was part of reality. But for theological students who were in touch with this trend of hermeneutics it was very easy to draw the conclusion that etymological misuse of words, contrary to their actual semantics in usage, was philosophically justifiable. In so far as the New Quest achieved something with its ideas of language, it is probably because in its actual operations it used this type of etymological interpretation rather little.[31]

The New Quest was of great interest to many because it was explicitly hermeneutic in emphasis and because the philosophy on which it was based was also hermeneutic in character. People thought that from this they could learn how to interpret the Bible. At times the will to achieve this overcame the force of common sense discrimination. There has been no more remarkable scene in modern theology than the rise of the Heidegger-Bultmann-Gadamer hermeneutical tradition to acceptance and popularity among people of conservative allegiance who are still furiously assaulting Bultmann for his skepticism, his demythologization program, and his strongly critical approach.[32] From any rational conservative approach this is surely foolishness: one cannot have Bultmann the hermeneutical expert without having also Bultmann the demythologizer, Bultmann the highly critical scholar, and the rest. But because the New Quest, and its allied hermeneutic offshoots, is so strongly directed towards the popular subject of hermeneutics, its concepts have had very wide circulation, and the picture of scholarship and historical study which it has used has come to be very widely disseminated. People who have not studied the literature or become acquainted with the personalities already see the scholarly tradition as a mass of "positivism;" interested only in the "objectivizing" of evidences and events.

Neither the original Quest, nor the New Quest, were good modes of entry into the search for canons of interpretation. In both cases the most prominent scholars concerned were talking not about interpretation as it normally takes place, as an activity between professor and student in the classroom face to face with a biblical text: they were arguing their own particular cases, urging their own theological solutions to ultimate problems. In the old Quest they were trying to argue their own solution to the question of the historical Jesus; in the New, perhaps the same, but also to a large extent arguing, through the example of the historical Jesus, the viability of a supposedly novel style of speech and thinking. But because of the centrality of their theme these discussions had greater influence on ideas of interpretation than they deserved to have.

As James Mays rightly saw, the question of how theological exegesis took place is a central problem for all understanding of the Bible. The twentieth century was very much aware of the need for a comprehension of the interpretative process. But, in the conditions of the twentieth century, it has been far from easy to achieve this. For the century began in a very confused theological mood, as a result of suggestions and proposals thrown up by the preceding century. The reactions to these difficulties were violent. It became characteristic for each theological generation to excommunicate the preceding one and its methods. Drastic responses became the order of the day. Abolition of natural theology, abolition of all apologetic discussion, abolition of all interest in the Jesus of history, denial of all relevance to historical study, and attempts to overthrow all the precedents of scholarship and replace them by some newly-thought-out scheme — all these became familiar phenomena. Much that was written, ostensibly about biblical interpretation, was really an attempt to justify a position about one of these matters. In order to understand how theological interpretation works we have to take a wide view, covering texts of all sorts and questions of all sorts, and not allow ourselves to be diverted by arguments that are really attempts to justify a particular theological position on this or that problem. For the carrying out of this purpose the thought of James Mays, deeply rooted in the experience of exegetical teaching, in a strong and sensible doctrinal tradition, and above all in reverence for the Bible itself, offers us exemplary guidance.

NOTES

1. This lecture was published as a separate item by Union Theological Seminary, Richmond.

2. On this see the exhaustive Excursus I on the Census of Quirinius in Schürer-Vermes-Millar, *The History of the Jewish People in the Time of Jesus Christ* (Edinburgh, T. and T. Clark, 1973), I, 399-428, which comes to the conclusion (p. 426) that "there is no alternative but to recognize that the evangelist based his statement on uncertain historical information."

3. *Affirmation* (Union Theological Seminary, Richmond), Vol. I, no. 7, December 1983, pp. 43-50; the passage quoted is on p. 45.

4. The works as quoted are well known: H. Bornkamm, *Jesus of Nazareth* (New York: Harper, 1960); Käsemann in *ZThK* 51, 1954, 125-53; English in *Essays on New Testament Themes* (London: SCM, 1964), pp. 15-47; Conzelmann, Ebeling and Fuchs in *ZThK* 56, 1959, Beiheft 1; Fuchs also in *ZThK* 53, 1956, 210-29; Conzelmann, article "Jesus Christus" in RGG³, 619-653; J.M. Robinson, *A New Quest of the Historical Jesus; and other Essays* (Philadelphia: Fortress, 1983 -earlier edition London, 1959); N.A. Dahl in *Kerugma und Dogma* I, 1955, 104-32; O. Michel in *EvTh* 15, 1955, 349-63; H.-W. Bartsch in *Theol. Exist. Heute* 78, 1960; Leander Keck, *A Future for the Historical Jesus* (Nashville: Abingdon, 1971). General bibliographical guidance in Robinson. More recent works include A.E. Harvey, *Jesus and the Constraints of History* (Philadelphia: Westminster, 1982); and the fact that Schillebeeckx wrote *two* great books, one called *Jesus* and the other called *Christ*, hardly fails to point to the liveliness of the question of the historical Jesus. For a completely negative view, which in any case pays no attention to the above literature, Cf. T.F. Torrance, "'The Historical Jesus' from the Perspective of a Theologian," in *The New Testament Age* (Bo Reicke Festschrift; Macon: Mercer University Press, 1984), II, 511-26.

5. *Princeton Seminary Bulletin* 6, 1985, p. 98.

6. Memoir of C.H. Dodd, *Proceedings* of the British Academy, 60, 1974; quotation from p. 12.

7. *Our Dialogue with Rome: the Second Vatican Council and After* (London; Oxford University Press, 1967), p. 50.

8. On the effects of this on our view of the old and New Quests, see below, note 24.

9. Cf. Michel, *op. cit.*, pp. 358ff.

10. These form chapters 2-4 of his *Jesus and the World of Judaism* (Philadelphia: Fortress, 1983).

11. Cf. *Jesus and the Language of the Kingdom* (Philadelphia: Fortress, 1976), p. 142.

12. This is brought out particularly well by Dahl, *op. cit.*

13. On Zoroaster see my recent discussion, "The Question of Religious Influence; the case of Zoroastrianism, Judaism and Christianity," in *JAAR* 53, 1985, 201-35; on his dates, see pp. 220f.

14. *Ibid.*, p. 99.

15. I quote from B.S. Childs, *The New Testament as Canon: an Introduction* (Philadelphia: Fortress, 1985), p. 537, but practically the same words could be found in a host of works.

16. On this see Robinson, *op. cit.*, pp. 22f., and works there discussed by him.

17. Cf. Tyrrell's *Christianity at the Cross-Roads* (London: Longmans, Green, 1913), p. 44.

18. Cf. *God was in Christ* (New York: Scribners, 1948), p. 56. For Baillie, writing at that time, Barthian and Bultmannian viewpoints could still be classified as closer than they later came to appear.

19. So Diem as reported by Robinson, p. 23.

20. Conzelmann, *ZThK, ibid.*, p. 4 and notes, says: "The dogmatic picture of Jesus is becoming transformed again into a historical, really a pseudohistorical, one," and cites as the strongest symbol of this the picture of Jesus given in Barth's *KD* IV/2. He goes on to maintain that at crucial points where Barth is contending for the historical facticity of the resurrection and the empty tomb his argumentation becomes purely historical-psychological in character.

21. According to Bartsch, *op. cit.*, p. 11, and note 30, Kähler's arguments on this side, i.e. those against the conservative-historical position, continue today to be fully valid.

22. Translated, edited and with an Introduction by Carl E. Braaten, (Philadelphia: Fortress, 1964); German original 1892.

23. The basic work is J.M. Robinson and J.B. Cobb, *The New Hermeneutic* (New York: Harper, 1964)

24. Cf., *A New Quest*, pp.9-10. Cf. also the quotations from Dodd and Caird, above, pp. 29f. It is likely that these expressions about the quest of the historical Jesus would be classified by Robinson as belonging to the old Quest. But the theological intentions in the minds of scholars such as they were quite different from the theological intentions for which the old Quest had been blamed. Note especially Caird's insistence that the quest belongs to and follows from the doctrine of the Incarnation. If this is really still the old Quest, then the reasons commonly alleged for dismissing the old Quest must be wrong; and, if they are wrong, that undermines the reason why there should be any New Quest at all. On Caird's

general theological and exegetical thoughts, see my Memoir of his life, to appear (1986?) in the *Proceedings* of the British Academy.

25. *The Two Horizons: New Testament Hermeneutics with Special Reference to Heidegger, Bultmann, Gadamer, and Wittgenstein*, (Grand Rapids: Wm. B. Eerdmans, 1980).

26. *A New Quest*, p. 67.

27. *Ibid.*, p. 68.

28. *Ibid.*, p. 67.

29. *Ibid.*, p. 28.

30. See my *Old and New in Interpretation* (London: SCM, 1966), in which (pp. 176ff.) I already criticized the way in which theologians, especially in the United States, accept the "positivistic" picture of nineteenth-century historiography, a picture which was largely a late American invention.

31. After all the shift in opinion in this matter, T.F. Torrance still thinks that he was right. In his *Reality and Evangelical Theology* (Philadelphia: Westminster, 1982), p. 160, note 18, he writes: "Barr's ill-judged attack on the lessons to be learned from etymology contrasts with Plato's wise judgement that we are often put on the right track of the objective semantic reference of a term by examining archaic forms (*Cratylus* 401C)." Plato: All that Torrance proves by this argument is his own inability to read Plato. The *Cratylus* is a satire in which it is shown how, from words, by "etymology," anything at all can be proved. Dogmaticians in any case know nothing about "archaic forms" and even less about the semantic consequences that they could draw from them if they did.

The matter of etymology, interestingly, worked in a paradoxical way. Though it was the "Bultmannian" rather than the "Barthian" and more conservative side of modern exegesis that was influenced by the Heideggerian tradition, Bultmann himself and many of his pupils knew language too well, and were too good as New Testament scholars, to try to do much within the Bible with the etymological fancies of Heidegger. It was more on the "Barthian" side, and in the more conservative strands of "Biblical Theology," that etymologizing exegesis was applied to biblical words. This was highly ironic. Etymology is usually justified as giving access to historical roots; but it was those who most opposed the theological value of historical investigation who found themselves most dependent on it. Thus both existentialism and historicism took a certain revenge on those who rejected them, and forced them to admit their dependence.

32. Cf. I. Howard Marshall (ed.), *New Testament Interpretation: Essays on Principles and Methods* (Grand Rapids: Eerdmans, 1977), and my review in *Theology* 1978, pp. 233-35.

THE CONTRIBUTION OF BIBLICAL THOUGHT TO AN UNDERSTANDING OF OUR REALITY*

by Claus Westermann
Translated by Donald G. Miller

The Creation

The Bible deals with the whole, the sum total of reality. To speak of God is to speak of totality. For this reason, the Bible begins with the creation of the world and the creation of mankind. The whole is thought of as an extension of space and time.

As the Bible in the very beginning speaks of the creation, it sets forth the totality of the creation. It speaks of the heavens, the earth and sea, of the wind and the clouds, of the trees and plants, of animal and man. That they are all creatures means: God has to do with all of them. If we confess "I believe in God, the creator of heaven and earth," and do not take seriously that every creature is related to God, that God has to do with all creatures, then this confession is an empty phrase. If for us there is a reality which does not have to do with God, then we do not know God, the Creator.

Again, the first chapter of the Bible speaks conjointly of the whole of creation as an extension in time. For this reason, the stories of the creation and the story of the flood belong together, they are complementary. The world has a beginning and the world has an end. Catastrophes belong to the history of the cosmos. The conclusion of the story of the flood means: From the beginning to the end, in spite of all catastrophes, the world is in God's hands. He alone who created it appoints its end: "I am the first and I am the last."

When it is a question of totality with regard to creation, there is only one single all-encompassing confrontation: God and the creation. Since the Enlightenment another has replaced this: man and nature. This new confrontation of man and nature, which also signifies totality, has resulted in seeing man as lord of nature. We now see what has resulted from this.

Reality as creation is so organized that everything, from the greatest to the smallest, remains a member of the creation. The fun-

*To Professor James Mays, my honored colleague at Union Seminary in Richmond, for his 65th birthday, with many good wishes. Given as a lecture in Munich, September 29, 1984.

damental organization is asserted in the Bible itself: the creation of the world and the creation of man are in the Bible independent events which later are for the first time united. The sciences participate in this fundamental organization of reality: they are organized into natural sciences and human sciences. The earlier organization into natural sciences and the arts corresponded to the Greek distinction between spirit and matter.

Whilst the sciences up to the late Middle Ages still had a distinct consciousness of working with one another in the whole of creation, they lost this consciuousness almost totally from the Renaissance and the Enlightemnent on. "Each one looked on his own way." Specialization resulted in an ever wider distancing from one another, and no centripetal force could stand against the centrifugal process. A mediating force could only have proceeded from the certainty that the world is a totality, that reality is entire. It could only have arisen by taking seriously the world as creation. The voice that could have said that was silent. In modern times the creation has had practically no significance for the Christian church; the church's learning and theology became specialized along with the other specialities. One heard nothing of a responsibility for the whole.

Now we face the result. Because in the sciences each has gone his own way, the earth as a dwelling place for man is threatened. This threat is rooted in the fact that among scientists there is no longer a concern about the totality of the related sciences and their technological effects on the whole world and the whole of mankind, but each is confined to his own specialty.

It is a good sign that now, finally, the evangelical and Catholic academies have seen it as a task of the church to make it possible for isolated sciences to enter into dialogue with one another; only sorrowfully this comes a century too late.

The Creation of Man

As the Bible relates the creation of man, it presents man, indeed man as he existed then and as he exists today, man as man, as he truly is. The customary representation is: God undertook to create man, and first made Adam out of dust and then Eve out of a rib of her husband. If one has this conception of the creation of man, he has not seriously listened to the story. This story clearly states: The one so produced is not really man! God pauses after he has created man; that is not man, the story continues, as the Creator intended. The narrator wishes to say: Man is really man first in community, with space required for life, provided with food and with a task, with work. Only with all this, or in all this, is he truly man. And he means by this not just one person of the primeval age, but in story form he is speaking of what pertains to contemporary human existence.

Hence, it is especially important for us today that mankind uphold the commission to cultivate and to preserve the earth, the space required for life in which God has placed him. By this the Creator has established the fundamental relation between man and nature: the task of cultivation and preservation. This commission given by the Creator, which is incumbent on the whole of mankind, has been disregarded. Mankind has let the garden go to ruin. That is our reality. The churches have not been aware of their neglect of the instructions of the Creator. They have not admonished and they have done nothing. Other movements were obliged to arise which have warned and are warning, which have done and are doing something.

Man was created in the image of God, says the creation story. On this the dignity of man is founded, a dignity which includes men of all nations, all races and all religions. As the storytellers began to speak of human rights, it was done in the firmly established belief that human rights rest on the dignity of man which his Creator conferred on him, that he created him in his own image. It would be well to reflect on the question why contemporary discussion of human rights is almost totally detached from faith in God the Creator.

The story of the creation of man is united with the story of the driving of man out of the garden. The storyteller here speaks not of an event which has taken place at a precise point in time. He speaks of contemporary man and intends to say that the destiny of man is indissolubly united with his limited existence. Man exists only between the limits of birth and death, he exists only within the limits which are set for him through his fallibility and his flawed nature. And this is here meant not only in a religious sense; it is true of men in the whole world and in all times. Real man is limited man. No glorification of man, no belief in progress, no philosophy of life, can alter this in the least. Because man is fallen, he is appointed to forgiveness. If the message of forgiveness stands at the very center of the Christian message, for the same reason it is necessary for the whole of mankind.

The Fathers

The Bible relates a history, and the history of God's people begins with the fathers. The narratives of the fathers revolve around a small life circle; here family and society were still one and the same. In this way the Bible calls attention to the fact that the smallest human community, the family, is the foundation of all others, and that this fundamental significance of the family will remain so long as mankind endures. All attempts to give to the state or the church or a class or the masses an absolute meaning bypasses reality. Each man has the imprint of the small, familial community on him and retains it throughout his entire life.

The distinct thing about the history of the fathers, however, is that here the family is plainly the community; they belong not to a race, a nation, a state or a church; they wander with their flocks from pasture to pasture. There is here no political, but only a family, authority; there are here no temple and no priests, no ministers and no prophets. The relation of individual men, and of this small group of men, to God is immediate, direct. When a word comes forth from God concerning a promise or an instruction, it comes directly to the father; the father and the members of the family invoke God out of their actual life experience. Everything that here takes place between God and this small group is a self-evident and inseparable constituent of their lives.

It is remarkable that the theologians of our time know nothing of this direct relation to God without any mediator, as it is presented in the history of the fathers. It is also remarkable that Luther, when he spoke of the priesthood of all believers, did not think of the fact that this was already expressed by the fathers. The Bible throughout knows of a relation to God which does not need a church or any other cultic institution.

Here is the place to speak of the understanding of miracle in the Bible, since wonder has a real significance for the first time in the history of the fathers.

In the Bible, miracle is an experience which a man or a group of men have with God. Much is told of this in the stories of the fathers, as is likewise true in the Gospels of the New Testament. It is with this that the story of Hagar deals when, with her small child on her arm, she wanders about in the desert, puzzled and with death from thirst staring her in the face. In her despair she lays her child under a bush, because she cannot bear to watch him dying, and withdraws, sits down and awaits death. Then comes a messenger of God and shows her a well of water close by, and the mother and her child are preserved.

This was for the fathers, in their hard life exposed to all sorts of dangers, an unforgettable experience. They told stories of such things, and these narratives were passed on in the group from generation to generation. That it was God who had rescued Hagar was for them self-evident. Because for her God was: he who can transform distress. God is the indispensable one.

This same thing is later declared in a large number of Psalms in which an individual man praises God who, standing by him in deadly peril, had delivered him out of the fangs of death. Behind each of these Psalms stands an abundance of similar experiences as Hagar had had in the wilderness. Miracle was experienced, not believed.

In the Bible miracle is just such an experience of deliverance from fatal distress, because of which God is praised and of which others are told. It has first of all nothing to do with faith. If one had questioned these men and women whether they believed in miracle, they would not at all have understood what was meant thereby. Miracles belonged to their personal experience, and were for them something most precious in that experience. Without such experiences of wonder life would have been desolate and dull. Miracles belonged in great measure to the reality of their lives. Miracle encountered one, one rejoiced over it and thanked God for it, one told others of it that they might rejoice with him.

If in western theology a conception of miracle arose little by little and became regnant, which understands a miracle as an event which overcomes or breaks through the laws of nature or as an act of God, this definition is not valid for the miracles narrated or reported in the Old and New Testaments. It cannot be conclusive for the reason that the men of whom these stories were told knew nothing of the idea of natural law; hence, they could not have thought of a divine miracle as a happening which broke through natural law. But this is essential: for them everything that happened in heaven and on earth, whether it be the arrangements by which the sun moves in its orbit or a young bird receives its nourishment, was effected by God. Why should God who has created all these arrangements violate them in order, through such violations, to prove himself God?

The Bible knows nothing of miracles as supernatural events. However, the people of God and individual men take delight in the fact that God does wonders: "Thou art the God who workest wonders" (Ps. 79:140). But the wonder of God remains an action in the sphere which for the men of the Bible is reality; hence, something like a supernatural wonder is not known in the Bible.

The Prophets

The prophets have neither predicted nor foretold. In their discourses, past, present and future come together. When the prophet announces the death of his king as the judgment of God, he then points to a present moment: "You have killed and robbed!" (cf. I Kings 21:17ff.). The prophets saw reality where the public reports had concealed or hushed it up, where the authorities out of fear kept silent.

For this reason prophecy is an indispensable ingredient of the Bible. Wherever God is spoken of, wherever the worship of God takes place, without at the same time the burning wrongs in the society in which the worship takes place being referred to candidly and by name, then the indictment against such false worship is as valid today as in the time of the prophets in which the indictments arose.

The prophets also saw and spoke out about reality in politics, without being inhibited by the state or the authorities. They saw the high and mighty, who had risen by conquest and subjugation of the little people, for what they truly are. In the powerful second chapter of the Book of Isaiah God's judgment is pronounced over all haughtiness and pride, precisely because it has soared so high. It is the same judgment out of which the earlier story of the tower of Babel arose.

The prophet Habakkuk saw the great powers in this fashion:

> Woe to the proud man, who never has enough, whose greedy gullet flings open as wide as Sheol and is as insatiable as death!(2:25)
>
> Woe to him who heaps up what is not his. . . and loads himself with pledges of debt!(2:6b)
>
> Woe to him who biulds a town with blood, and founds a city on iniquity!(2:12)
>
> Yes, the stone in the wall cries out and the beam in the woodwork replies to him.(2:11)
>
> He catches everything with his fishhook, he drags it in his net and gathers it in his seine.(1:15a, b) Therefore he sacrifices to his net and burns incense to his seine.(1:16a)
>
> He makes his own might his God.(1:11b)*

In powerful empires which arose through conquest, the prophets saw not greatness but *hubris.* They saw and passed sentence on reality.

* Translation of these passages made from the German Text.

The Psalms

In the Psalms man speaks to God exactly as he is and as he thinks. If in the main they are organized according to lamentation and praise psalms, this corresponds to the life of men which unfolds in the polarity of sorrow and joy. One speaks to God just as he feels, lament being the speech of sorrow, praise the speech which directs joy to God. Also, when a man in view of grievous sorrow can no longer understand God, the Psalms offer the possibility to direct questions of accusation against God: Why? How long? By separating lamentation from prayer in the Christian tradition, prayer has lost an essential aspect of reality.

In the midst of the Old Testament Psalms of lamentation stands the confession of confidence, which represents the transition from lament to petition; therefore it often begins with "But." "But you are my confidence," "on you I rely." Hereby are heaped up the comparisons which point out what God means to the one praying in his sorrow: "You are my rock," "you are my fortress," "my feast in the time of need," "I hide myself under the shadow of your wings," and many others. Once one reflects on these comparisons with the question in mind, "What did these mean outside this association with prayer?" he discovers that each of them tells a story or alludes to what had happened in an experience of an earlier time before these Psalms had appeared, an event which is authenticated by these words. Some time ago I assembled every comparison which appears in the 150 Psalms and arranged them according to the spheres of profane life from which they proceeded. I saw there something that I had never seen before: the comparisons in the Psalms bespeak the whole of reality in which the people of Israel lived. Every sphere of existence appears in the comparisons; and that explains the liveliness and power of the Psalms through the centuries and the millenia. The whole of reality is expressed in the prayers of the Psalms.

If in the words of confidence in the Psalms God is represented and invoked as the indispensable One, if the Psalms of praise report that he has turned away the distress of a man and that this man has taken this experience with him into his ongoing life, then this becomes clear: One must not first believe in God in order to be able to pray to him; prayer to God is for every human being an open standing possibility, because God is necessary and has turned away sorrow. He belongs to the reality of a human life as much as inhalation and exhalation. One can call on God. He is necessary.

The Wisdom Literature

Wisdom is based on the creation. God has so created man that he can find his way in the world in which God has set him, that he can control the life which he leads in this world. To this end God has given him intelligence. But wisdom is more than intelligence. Wisdom is the product of maturity. A wisdom saying which is handed down as a tradition is the product of such maturity, a fruit of reflection on reality, which can be a guide to others. In the Wisdom literature common sense receives its biblical dignity. Not only the speaking of God but also reflective language about profane reality maintains its place in the canon. The reality of man and his world—wholly apart from man's relation to God—is to be taken seriously as a creation of God. This is confirmed by the fact that no small part of Jesus' words in the Gospels are words from the ancient Israelite folk wisdom.

I will point out by three examples in what way biblical wisdom unobtrusively challenges us to take reality seriously and to accept it just as it is.

At the beginning stands the Preacher:

> For everything there is a season, and a time for every
> matter under heaven:
>> a time to be born, and a time to die;
>> a time to plant, and a time to pluck up what is planted;
>> a time to kill, and a time to heal;
>> a time to break down, and a time to build up;
>> a time to weep, and a time to laugh;
>> a time to mourn, and a time to dance;
>> a time to cast away stones, and a time to gather stones together;
>> a time to embrace, and a time to refrain from embracing;
>> a time to seek, and a time to lose;
>> a time to keep, and a time to cast away;
>> a time to rend, and a time to sew;
>> a time to keep silence, and a time to speak;
>> a time to love, and a time to hate;
>> a time for war, and a time for peace.
>> —Ecclesiastes 3:1-8

I will speak little of these words of wisdom. Each one who perceives that this is wisdom can himself draw from this word and ever anew reflect on it. I will say but one thing: this is a passionately polemic word. The wise man directs his attack against all wise-acres who would make a principle out of one side of these alternatives. He has grasped the fact that existence is being in time, that there is reality only in these polar rhythms. It cannot be reduced to timeless principles.

The second example is furnished by the Book of Job. Job's

friends are representatives of a pious wisdom which sought to establish itself on timeless principles. They said: the fate of the devout must be a blessed one; the wicked must lead a cursed life. Therefore Job must be a transgressor. To this Job answered at the end of the dialogue: you can well see that reality differs from your teaching.

> Why do the wicked live, reach old age, and grow mighty in power? (21:7)
>
> Their houses are safe from fear, and no rod of God is upon them. (21:9)
>
> Have you not asked those who travel the roads, and do you not accept their testimony that the wicked man is spared in the day of calamity . . . ? (21:29,30)
>
> How then will you comfort me with empty nothings? There is nothing left of your answers bur falsehood.(21:34,9,29,30,34)

Here the teaching of the friends stands against both reality and experience. A teaching about God which resists reality is worthless: "Your maxims are proverbs of ashes"(13:12a)!

A third example: the early Israelite wisdom is not a teaching in which one who is more wise instructs another who is less wise. It is comprised of short sayings which one can recall and on which he may meditate. They speak to men come of age and summoned to free, independent judgment; the conclusions therefrom call each person to account.

There is a group of sayings which consist only of a comparison; human conduct is compared with an example in its surroundings:

> Lips of knowledge — a precious jewel
> Many a rash word wounds like a sword thrust
> Like vinegar poured on a wound — he who sings songs to a
>   heavy heart
> A word spoken at the right time — a golden apple in a silver
>   bowl
> A proverb in the mouth of fools — a thorn branch stuck into
>   the hand of a drunkard
>   - cf. Proverbs 20:15b, 12:18a, 25:20, 25:11, 26:9

Each of the above-mentioned comparisons in the surrounding world should speak of a distinct relation and should serve as a judgment over this relationship. The proverbs have the same function which ethics, or moral teaching, has in another cultural situation. Here it is opposed to a judgment of human behavior based on timeless principles or on bypassing realities.

The Parables

The parables of Jesus point the hearers to the reality in which they live. When Jesus relates a parable, perchance the parable of the sower, he does not tell it so that the hearers will believe on him, but that they will reflect on it: "He who has ears to hear, let him hear!" The hearer himself should independently form a judgment on what Jesus meant by this parable. But the interpretation of a parable is never exhaustive; one finds a meaning, which serves only for further reflection; but no interpretation can be final. There are also interpretations of the parables taken up in the tradition, such as those in the parable of the various soils. These do not stem from Jesus, but from those who have reflected on them. Also, in their interpretation they have not expressed the chief point: that Jesus speaks in this parable of God's power of blessing, as in the parable of the sower. Jesus intends to say that there is an activity of God which manifests itself not in word and faith, not in supplication and granting of requests, not in challenge and decision, but in a silent activity which consists simply in that something grows. What issues from this may be very different and one can also have very different opinions about it. But the essential thing that the parable wishes to say is: God can make something grow, in the fields, in a school, in the thoughts of a man, in a community. But in regard to this, man himself can do absolutely nothing. If this silent growth is not bestowed, then no life is produced.

Reality should confirm what Jesus tells his hearers concerning God. He points in his parable to the reality which surrounds them—in the flowers and the wind, in the trees and the field, in the social life of men and in their work, in the handicraft and work of farmers and many others. What he has to say to men about God embodies this reality of life which is not far from men. What happens between a master and his servant, a father and his son, a man and his property, all certainly belong to the creation of God, and are not foreign to the action and speech of God.

This insight is not grasped in the customary understanding of the parables. Rather, some spiritual essence or rational inference is sought, the so-called *tertium comparationes*, and when it is found the parable has no further use and one can himself, with the help of his own perception, expand upon this spiritual essence. Consequently, the parables are completely misunderstood. Had that been the purpose of Jesus in narrating the parables, he could have made it much easier for himself and his hearers and would have said precisely what one can draw from the parables.

All parables are little stories. Jesus spoke the parables so that the stories *as such* could speak to us. The story, however, can never be replaced by a moral which one may draw from it; it can only say what it intends to say as a whole, from the first to the last sentence. The parable story is the abiding reality, not our interpretation.

This has a very far-reaching consequence. In the parables, when Jesus speaks of God he gives a little slice out of our reality the honor of speaking along with him. Once one reflects thereon, it becomes clear that the creation of God, our total reality as God has created it, has a much weightier and much richer voice in the Bible than those passages which speak expressly about creation. The entire vast abundance of comparisons, in the Old Testament as in the New, speaks along with any talk about God.

The parables of Jesus can best show us this: what the Bible says of God is deeply imbedded in the reality of our world, our life, our thoughts and feelings. It is not the fault of the Bible if, in modern times, it has become more and more foreign to modern man, further and further removed from his reality. It is rather the result of a Western tradition of theology and the speech and practice which have issued from it, which have been governed by a predisposition toward abstract ideas and an abstract methodology. The result of this has been that the simple, most anecdotal idiom of the Bible, which has a predominately verbal structure, has been recoined into one of abstract substantives and a terminology on a higher level determined by Greek speculation.

We can no longer afford this estrangement between the Bible and reality in an epoch when the whole of mankind is threatened by dangers which haunt us all. It is high time that we turn back to the simple idiom of the Bible which is closely related to reality.

PROPHECY AS LITERATURE:
A RE-APPRAISAL

by Ronald S. Clements

The phenomenon of ancient Israelite prophecy is known to us today through the corpus of writings preserved in the second part of the Old Testament canon. This consists of the Former and Latter Prophets, but it is this second part, the Latter Prophets, which contains an amazingly rich collection of prophetic sayings and records of prophetic experiences originating over a period of more than three centuries. This body of prophetic writings is wholly unique, in its form as well as in its character, since nowhere else from antiquity has there been preserved such a literary collection. As features of a very widely occurring religious activity prophecy and divination were essentially oral in their character and belonged within an oral spoken framework of communication. Even when it had become accepted for prophecies to be written down and oracular utterances and sign-words recorded in order to be read, this fundamental oral setting was only very partially modified. It is in accord with this that the most popular forms of oracular utterance and divination, or dream interpretation, were brief and closely related to the context in which they were initially given.[1] A prophetic literature, therefore, on the scale that the Old Testament has preserved for us, in which long series of prophetic sayings are brought together, remains a wholly unique product of ancient Israel's religious tradition.

It has been a consistent feature of the modern critical study of this prophetic literature since the beginning of the nineteenth century to endeavor to penetrate behind this literary form of prophecy in order to recreate its original historical context where its oral nature prevailed. The goal of critical interpretation ever since the work of J.G.Herder and J.G. Eichhorn has been to "hear" the word of prophecy as it was originally proclaimed.[2] To this extent the literary form of prophecy has been regarded as both a help and a hindrance. It is a help, since without it we should not know of the prophecy at all, but it has been looked upon also as a hindrance since it often obscures the proper authentic setting in which the saying was first given. However, it is abundantly clear, as a number of fresh critical studies have noted, that the literary form of prophecy in the Old Testament establishes not simply a medium of preservation, but also a medium of interpretation. Written prophecy is necessarily different from oral prophecy precisely because it is written and is thereby made subject to the gains and losses that written fixation entails. The purpose of this essay is, therefore, to explore some of the issues that are raised by the transition from oral to written prophecy and in particular to argue that these issues are far more central to the understanding of prophecy than has customarily been allowed.

Literary Aspects of the Prophetic Tradition

Attention to the written form of the prophetic literature has been stimulated during recent years by two main currents of biblical research. First of all, it almost goes without saying that the aims of canon criticism - to accept and interpret the biblical text in the form in which it now exists - have inevitably raised afresh the question of how we are to understand the complex structure of the four great prophetic books, Isaiah, Jeremiah, Ezekiel, The Book of the Twelve.[3] For Judaism, as for the early Christian church, written prophecy existed primarily in this canonical form and this had inevitable consequences for the way in which it was interpreted. Prophecies could be drawn indiscriminately from any part of the established canon and assumed to proclaim a coherent message such as we see, for instance, at Qumran and in the way in which New Testament writers make use of prophetic sayings. Without wishing to raise questions here about the degree of authority which we should accord to the canonical form of prophecy, we may be content to note that this form is an indispensable prerequisite for understanding how prophecy came to be used and understood by Jews and Christians. The canonical form of the prophetic literature is also important for understanding how and why certain assumptions came to be made about its authorship.

Alongside canon criticism, however, we must also note the great importance of redaction criticism as a stimulus to questioning how and why prophecy exists as a literature. The processes of literary growth, from smaller to larger units, may appear at times to have been a random process, and even little more than an accident of transmission and preservation. Closer examination, however, shows that this was not often, or even normally, the case and that intricate structures were planned and imposed upon the smaller units of material. Even so complex a composition as the Book of Isaiah, which evidently took centuries to reach its final form, shows

evidence that, through its many stages of growth, intentional connections and interrelationships between the parts were planned.
Such larger compositional units, with the possibilities which they
present for pointing to significant theological aims, have only been
rendered possible because of the written fixation of prophetic
oracles.

It is noteworthy that a most recent avenue of research into the
prophetic texts has made use of rhetorical criticism to draw attention to structural connections and poetic artifices which embrace
quite substantial literary blocks of material.[4] So, for instance, M.
Greenberg's "holistic" pattern of interpretation of Ezekiel 1-20 has
recognized compositional unity where earlier critics had noted
more heavily the distinctions and separateness of units of
material.[5] Not least, however, it must be noted that the literary
fixation of prophecies has undoubtedly provided a fundamental
datum for the formulation of new prophecies. So the "New Song of
the Vineyard" in Isaiah 27:2-6 has been composed with conscious
reference to the original Isaianic "Song of the Vineyard" in Isaiah
5:1-7, [6] and this is merely one example of a whole range of
elements in the prophetic writings where later prophecies have been
built upon, and related to, earlier ones. Although, therefore, it is
clear that there is a great deal of material in each of the four major
prophetic books which can be described as "redactional" in the
literary sense of having been added by an editor to assist the reader,
there is also much that must be regarded as genuinely new prophecy, even though it has been based upon an earlier written one. Ultimately this was to give rise to a vast range of commentary material which sought to interpret old prophecies in relation to much
later events, a process that is in some measure still with us. Even so,
we must insist that there is no clear line of demarcation between the
work of an editor and the work of a prophet, since the former, too,
can fulfil a truly prophetic function in the way in which earlier
prophecies are handled.

A number of recent studies from the perspectives of Social Anthropology have concentrated attention upon the great impact that
literacy has had upon ancient society.[7] So far as the rise of epic
narrative is concerned, it is evident that written form made possible
a vastly extended and enriched type of literary composition. The
short anecdotal narratives which could be recounted orally became
interconnected into much lengthier compositions with the opening
of many new possibilities for the intrusion of plots and subplots. At
the same time, the greater length that became easily accommodated

into written narratives imposed new restraints and demands in the interests of consistency and coherence. Undoubtedly other forms of entertainment and instruction which had their origins in oral tradition were compelled to submit to the demands of a stricter measure of editorial control and shaping once they were committed to writing. We can easily extend this list to indicate how literacy influenced and shaped all kinds of narrative and didactic compositions, and thereby inevitably served to change the patterns and disciplines of human thinking.[8] The possibility of constant reference back to an original proposition or starting-point and the opportunity provided by written preservation for delayed reflection and examination, both served to impose new controls over thought and artistry. The wider implications of this for the impact of literacy upon the powers and processes of human reasoning, and for the gains and losses which it imposed upon artistic forms, are only just beginning to be extensively examined and range far beyond the scope of this essay. Nevertheless we may maintain that prophecy too, as a widespread and popular feature of religious activity, was profoundly influenced and changed by its preservation in written form.

We may recognize that prophecy consisted, at an elementary level, in a pronouncement of a divine message by a recognized individual. The prophet served as a messenger of the gods, or of God. Such a message usually contained some disclosure of the divine attitude, or intention, most often backed up with a fuller explanation of the reason for this. It is then not difficult to see how, once a sequence of prophecies were brought together and preserved in writing, they could be examined and reflected upon as to their consistency and in regard to the possibility of extracting from them some fuller understanding of the divine nature and purpose. In a very real measure, therefore, a genuine prophetic theology only became possible once prophecy had acquired written fixation. It is in this respect that the significance of the differences between oral and written prophecy come most fully to the fore. On the one hand it is true that, when a prophet delivers a divine message, he presupposes some understanding of the divine nature. It is this aspect of prophecy, with its enquiry into the assumed implications concerning the divine purpose which the prophet's utterance presumes, which constituted the central theological feature of Old Testament prophecy for B. Duhm.[9] There is undoubtedly an element of truth in this assumption, since how the prophet thought of God's nature inevitably served to shape his understanding of the divine intention. It is our contention, however, that it was not until a whole corpus of prophetic sayings came into being as a written record that it became possible and necessary to look for a larger degree of coherence and consistency in their implied disclosure of the divine nature and a genuine theology became possible.

It is precisely because the two essential preconditions for the constructing of such a theological understanding of God were present in ancient Israel that this process of "theologizing" on the basis of prophetic utterances became so important. These were that all the prophecies so brought together should be regarded as emanating from the same deity and that this deity should be regarded as possessing a completely consistent and unchanging nature. These conditions were undoubtedly present in Israel, with its strong monotheising tendency. We may argue, therefore, that prophecy was of the greatest importance for the rise of a genuine theology, not because each prophet presupposed a distinct cultic tradition, as G. von Rad has so strongly stressed, nor because each prophet unconsciously reveals his own inner picture of God, as B. Duhm argued more than a century ago.[10] Rather it is that the bringing together of a variety of different prophetic sayings, some given from the same prophet at different times and others from a variety of prophets of different periods, raised fundamental issues about the integrity and consistency of the one divine Being who was understood to have brought Israel into existence and to have planned its destiny. To this extent we must insist that the true groundwork of theology, seen in a biblical context, is not simply a matter of drawing together a number of distinct divine attributes - justice, righteousness, holiness, mercy, and so on which are commonplace in most ancient (and modern) religious traditions, but of showing how they can cohere in a single divine Being. It is this aspect which is so strikingly present in the Old Testament and so dramatically highlighted by the canonical corpus of prophecy. God is both just and merciful, as appears in most human religious traditions, but the more profound dimension of genuine theologizing only appears when a given range of human experiences are interpreted in the light of this justice and mercy. This calls for a more profound level of reasoning than simply to regard painful experiences as divine acts of judgment and pleasurable ones as acts of godly kindness and mercy.

A further feature may be raised in consideration of an earlier phase of scholarly research into the questions of oral and written preservation of the prophetic traditions of the Old Testament. This concerns the fact that such discussion centred largely upon questions of accuracy and fidelity of transmission of the sayings of particular prophets.[11] Once it came to be widely argued that, since prophecy was essentially a proclaimed medium of divine message-giving it was preserved orally before being committed to writing, matters of accuracy and authenticity in respect of oral tradition loomed large in scholarly discussion. Although interesting and illuminating comparisons can be made from the careful study of other religious traditions outside the Old Testament, no hard and fast general conclusions can be drawn. Oral transmission may, given certain conditions, be very accurate, but there is no necessity to suppose that it was always so in ancient communities. In this regard the debate that has now largely been exhausted about oral and literary aspects of the transmission of Old Testament prophecy offered few firm conclusions. Our present concern, however, is not directly with these questions of the accuracy and fidelity of oral transmission.

This earlier period of scholarly discussion served to bring firmly to the fore a picture of ancient prophetic activity that has had widespread repercussions for understanding the complex character of the prophetic books of the Old Testament. Ever since the work of critical scholarship in the late nineteenth century the need for distinguishing between "original" and "secondary" elements in the prophetic writings has proved one of the most prominent, as well as most controversial, features of their interpretation. The matter of authenticity has proved to be a very important, if often unanswerable, question, even, at times, of passages of central significance. The belief in a period of oral transmission has served to offer one possible avenue of explanation for this. On the assumption that the great prophetic individuals gave rise to small schools of disciples, whose existence continued long after the original prophet's death, it has been possible to argue that our major prophetic books, especially those of Isaiah and Ezekiel, are the products of prophetic schools.[12] Hence, the tradition of the original prophet's sayings was combined with further elaborations of them and their supplementation by new ones until the conglomerate of primary and secondary elements which our books now contain was reached. In this reconstruction of the activity of prophetic schools in ancient Israel an explanation is offered for the agency of transmission of the original prophet's sayings, at first orally and then in writing, as well as their supplementation by a great deal of secondary material, which may nevertheless be regarded as genuinely prophetic. Furthermore, in spite of the corporate origin of the extant book bearing the prophet's name, it may be regarded as deeply marked by his authoritative and authorial stamp. The wider implications of this reconstruction of how at least two of the prophetic books came into being need not detain us here, except to note that such a view presupposes that oral transmission and authorship traditions may serve to some extent to explain each other.

The Foundations of Prophetic Literature

We cannot ignore the fact that the processes by which the first written prophetic collections were made are not at all clear. Only in the case of one prophet, Jeremiah, do we have a detailed tradition concerning how a written collection of his prophecies came to be made (Jer.36). Even here questions have been raised as to the reliability of the tradition concerning this account of how the written collection of these prophecies came to exist. In part the story is aetiological, serving to explain how the word of God was rejected by the king Jehoiachin and how the prophet responded to this by committing his prophecies to writing a second time.[13] The initial reason for Jeremiah's inability to deliver his divinely given message in person is not made wholly clear (Jer.36:5), but is intelligible enough. Whatever explanatory purposes the story has now been a-dapted to serve, its authentic historical basis in events can be perfectly reasonably accepted. What is especially striking is that the date given for this action - the fourth year of Jehoiachin (605/4 B.C.) - is remarkably late in Jeremiah's career if his call to prophesy came in 627/6 B.C. (Jer. 1:2). However, there would appear to be good reason for accepting as reliable both the date of the prophet's call and the date of the first written collection of his prophecies, since there is no reason to suppose that from the beginning a prophet would naturally wish to have all his prophecies written down. In this case it would appear to have been the restraints imposed upon the prophet, and his anticipated expectation of the rejection of his words, which serve to offer a reason why the choice of establishing a written collection of his prophecies was made. To what extent we should regard Baruch as a deeply committed personal disciple of the prophet, or as a professional scribe, may be left aside.

Here we are called upon to raise the larger question of the extent to which literacy may be presupposed as a widely employed accomplishment in ancient Israel. Clearly Israel was a semiliterate society since writing had been known for centuries, and, where appropriate, written documents and written messages were commonplace. The discovery of the Lachish letters from the time of Jeremiah is sufficient evidence of this. Why, however, should some prophetic messages be written down and others not? Clearly it was not simply the contemporary reaction to their poetic and religious excellence which occasioned this, but rather the dire nature of the events which they foretold which occasioned such preservation. A.H.J. Gunneweg has suggested that prophets, being closely linked to the centres of cultic life, would have had ready access to literary skills and reason enough for attaining and devoloping them.[14] Yet it would appear that more than this was involved and that the official rejection of Jeremiah's message, and the restraints imposed on him as a prophet, were primary factors in forcing him to adopt a literary preservation of his prophetic words. A closely comparable situation to this appears to have existed for Isaiah at the time of the Syro-Ephraimite crisis and provides the most obvious explanation for the composition of Isaiah's "Memoir" of his prophecies from this time (cf. Isa. 8:16f.).[15] We can then note still further in respect of Amos that, although the event does not have any explicit connection with the writing down of prophecies from him, the rejection of his message and of his prophetic role in Bethel forms a central biographical event in his activity. There are powerful circumstantial features which indicate, therefore, that in the cases of Amos, Isaiah and Jeremiah it was the experience of rejection, and a refusal on the part of governmental authority to heed the message given which compelled each of these men to resort to written recording of the pronouncements given.

These points are of very considerable significance when we come to consider the reasons for a transition from oral to written prophecy and the likely factors which must have operated in the manner and circumstances of such a change. It is almost too obvious to point out that, in a broad historical context, it was the impact of Assyrian and Babylonian imperial expansion upon Israel, with Israel's consequent loss of national freedom and national identity, which provided the primary stimulus for preserving prophecies dealing with these events. It is noteworthy, then, to consider that a prophecy preserved in writing must be regarded as significantly affected once events have taken place which can be regarded as fulfilling its forewarnings of doom. The prophecy has been "confirmed" by divine action, and has undoubtedly acquired new status and authority as a result of this.[16] At the same time, not only is the prophecy itself deeply affected, but the situation of those who read it in the wake of such events would have inevitably differed greatly from the circumstances of those who first heard the prophet declare it publicly. Nor should we suppose that the prophet himself would have felt satisfaction in being proved right. On the contrary, he had in a measure failed, since his hearers had not heeded the warnings that God had given to them. The situation of those who read the prophet's words in the light of events, even granting that they had been preserved exactly in the form in which he had given them, was no longer the same situation that had prevailed for those who had originally heard him. In a sense, the readers of the written collection may be regarded as the victims of the events which had taken place when the prophet's original hearers had rejected him and his message. This alone can assist us in understanding the very heavy interest in the theme of rejection of God's word which colors the prophecies of Jeremiah in particular, but others also to varying degrees. Nor is it altogether out of place to suggest that, if a sense of the prophet's having been rejected by his contemporaries but nevertheless having been proved right by events belongs to the essence of written prophecy, this will have influenced what was preserved. The concern would have been less to record accurately and precisely what the original prophet's words had been at the time when he gave them, and more carefully to show how they had fallen on deaf ears through human sinfulness and obstinacy. This is in no way to concede the kind of exaggerated and extreme claims that all prophecy must be understood as really a *post eventum* product of communities trying to understand their painful present. Rather the genuineness of the prophet's warnings and threats would appear to be unassailable. Neverthwless a measure of truth must be allowed to those recent critics who have drawn attention to the later editorial interests which colored the preserved prophetic texts.[17]   The earlier prophecies are necessarily being remembered in the light of events which have subsequently taken place.

A further factor must also be taken into consideration. Although there was a measure of *ad hoc* particularism about what a prophet said in a specific situation, there was a necessary requirement of a prophet, if he were to retain credibility, that he should be consistent and that his message should presuppose a consistent picture of the divine nature and intentions. A prophet could not be constantly changing his message and its implications, even though his audiences and their situations would inevitably change. We have already remarked that this is one of the most marked ways in which sayings recorded in writing are affected by their written preservation. It becomes possible to reflect upon, and if practicable to harmonize, the implications of each separate saying. To this extent it became possible, in the formation of written prophetic collections, to conjoin ideas and themes which the prophet had given at different times in order to establish a more comprehensive whole. As all critical examination of the over-all structure of the major prophetic collections has demonstrated, neither chronology nor thematic connectedness can provide a total and inclusive explanation for the way in which the separate prophecies have been brought together. At best they serve as only a partial basis for unravelling the reasons for the complex structure of the books.

All of this points us to recognize the serious limitations of a type of interpretation of prophecy which is concerned only to hear what the prophet said at the time when he originally said it. Certainly this should by no means be dismissed as an unimportant and unworthy goal, but it may often be beyond the powers of critical scholarship to do more than arrive at an approximation of this. Even more, it will undoubtedly fail to explain a great deal of other material which is to be found in the prophetic literature. To a not inconsiderable degree the situation of the readers for whom these sayings had been written down in a more or less permanent form was different from the situation of the first hearers. Furthermore, even the situation of the first readers would not have prevailed indefinitely but would have undergone progressive changes. As prophecies continued to be read in the light of contemporary events so all kinds of devices came to be employed to give them a more contemporary relevance. Included among such devices was a growing need to concentrate upon the more timeless aspects of religious life and spiritual duties. So such themes as unquestioning obedience and fidelity to Yahweh, adherence to the *torah*, often without specifying what form this *torah* took, rejection of idolatry and waiting for God's ultimate vindication of his people, all combined to give to written prophecy a more "timeless" character. Over-all we may claim that the tension between a historical particularism, dictated by the origin of prophecy in specific historical and politically defined situations, and a religious timelessness, determined by the need of succeeding generations to continue reading, and learning from, preserved prophecies marks the most prominent concern in its interpretation.

Prophetic Literature and Prophetic Theology

We may attempt to draw certain basic guidelines from these considerations for a useful modern goal of biblical interpretation.

Not least here we must affirm at least a relative measure of endorsement to the principle of canon criticism. We may do this on two counts: first the canonical shaping of the four great collections of the Latter Prophets has undoubtedly arisen on the basis of deep and genuine concerns for the preservation and understanding of prophecy. No doubt this could be sufficiently taken care of in the province of redaction criticism, if the interpreter simply retains a concern to understand the form and structure of the extant text. Yet this leads us to consider the second point that needs to be made here. There are marked similarities and connections, at times amounting to explicit cross references, between the various prophetic books. It would appear to be a highly misleading model to suppose that each of the prophetic collections was formed independently of the others, and that each took shape without reference to the others. The degree of interconnectedness is such as to show that this was not the case.[18] It would appear to be necessary therefore, if the prophetic books are truly to be understood as a fundamental part of the literature of the Old Testament, that the social, political and religious context which affected all of these books should be properly taken into account. So, for example, the reasons why prophecies threatening doom and judgment are so often brought to a conclusion by words of hope - a phenomenon that affects all of the collections to varying degrees -can scarcely be resolved by looking for independent explanations in each separate case. The fact that this recurs with sufficient frequency to manifest itself as a pattern suggests that it is the same basic needs that have prompted this redactional activity throughout the prophetic corpus. So also the shift towards a more apocalyptic type of prophecy, which is most evident in Isaiah and the Book of the Twelve, would point us in the same direction. The growth of a kind of corpus of authoritative prophetic literature would appear, therefore, to have been taking place alongside, and in conjunction with, the shaping of the individual prophetic books.

This raises the further question, of greatest interest to any quest for a prophetic theology, concerning the extent to which messages given by one prophet have been affected by messages given through other prophetic figures. Once the concern with the genius of each individual prophetic personality had become important to the modern interpretation of prophecy in the wake of the German Enlightenment, then clearly the concern with authenticity was a matter of very real and deep theological importance. Yet such was not the view of the ancients, if we may judge from the kind of literature which has been preserved for us. Since prophecy was a message, or series of messages, from God, then not only was it reasonable to look for some kind of consistency and coherence in the sayings of each individual prophet, but also across the whole spectrum of prophecy. The very natural assumption was undoubtedly present among those who preserved and interpreted prophecy to believe that God must be consistent with himself. This, of course, allowed fully for differences of emphasis in particular situations, but assumed that God's over-all plan and intentions for his people, and for all nations, must be a consistent one. It would certainly appear to have been the case that some of the minor inconsistencies which manifest themselves in each prophetic book have really been occasioned by the desire to achieve this larger consistency in the presentation of God's plans, especially where these related directly to the future hope and expectations of Israel in Diaspora.

Nor can we leave this matter aside without noting its significance for the changing distinctions that emerged in the understanding of "true" and "false" prophecy. Initially a simple formula relating to the way in which a prophecy was, or was not, confirmed by events appeared sufficient to explain this (cf. Deut.18:21f.). Alongside this it became more and more important to extend these distinctions to take account of more factors than just this single historical one, as Deut. 13:1-5 shows. In the still larger perspective of the emergence of a substantial corpus of prophetic literature after the exile it would certainly have been essential to achieve, even if at times through rather strained literary devices, a consistent picture of what the prophetic hope entailed. This too, therefore, would have intruded itself as a major factor in helping to shape these documents into their final form and in compelling the abandonment of prophecies that could no longer be brought into such a scheme. False prophecy came to be understood in terms of a larger range of (proto-canonical) assumptions concerning the reasons for Israel's past failure and the contents of its future hope. At the same time, if we may judge from the complexities of the verbal imagery and interpreted metaphors to be found in apocalyptic, the pressure grew for maintaining considerable flexibility in the understanding of what the authoritative canonical tradition of prophecy foretold. The theological interpretation of prophecy, therefore, must undoubtedly be open to the way in which prophecy was affected by the canonical context in which it has now been preserved. This not only concerns the growth of the separate prophetic books in a redaction critical perspective but also the ways in which the shaping of the prophetic corpus as a whole has left its impress upon each of the separate collections.

There is, however, a further theological consideration of major importance for the understanding of ancient Israelite prophecy in its preserved form. This concerns the relationship between its pronouncements of doom and judgment, with the invective employed to sustain this, and the declarations of hope and coming salvation which appear within it at many levels. The earlier critical perspective, which viewed the fall of Jerusalem in 587 B.C. and the experience of the Babylonian exile as providing the dividing line between the message of doom and the message of hope, clearly possessed a kind of commonsense persuasiveness. That it represents an oversimplification and succeeds only in telescoping together a much more varied and fluctuating series of political and historical developments should now be conceded. Nevertheless, it does contain a substantial element of truth, since it was clearly in the wake of the catastrophe of 587 B.C. that Israel came to believe that the nadir of its fortunes had passed. The paradox is fully apparent, therefore, that, in spite of such extensive retention of pronouncements of coming doom, backed up by appropriate invective, the corpus of prophetic writings as a whole is profoundly and firmly hopeful in its message. The message of doom serves both to explain the past, in the manner of a theodicy, to warn and admonish the present, since Israel is seen to be living under the consequences of its past experiences of judgment, and to provide a groundwork of hope for the rich and glorious future. From the perspective of the editors of these prophetic collections it would have appeared more essential that the larger theological (prophetic) context should have been kept in the reader's attention than that each separate historical context should have been fully made clear. In consequence, the pattern of bringing even the most fearful of warnings and threats to a hopeful conclusion by words of reassurance and hope would appear to reflect the theological and literary needs of the prophetic redactors rather than a startling ambivalence in what an individual prophet proclaimed in the face of the various crises which his hearers confronted. This is not to seek to return to the older dogmatism which insisted that all prophecies of hope must be postexilic. Rather it is to try to understand the fact that, in preserving a collection of written prophecies, the scribes and editors who have done so were endeavoring to serve a wider range of concerns and religious purposes than simply to observe a kind of biographical exactitude which ensured that each literary unit matched precisely the occasion in the prophet's activity in which it had originated. So much confusion has arisen and strained interpretation has been encouraged as a result of this false assumption that the redactional aims of those who have given us the prophetic books of the Old Testament were primarily biographical.

It may not be out of place in this respect to suggest that the frequently adopted assumption that historical and literary questions must first be settled before useful theological insights can be gained may all too readily ignore the deep interconnectedness of all three. Nor can it be ignored that, as we begin more fully to explore the religious and editorial interests which have helped to shape our prophetic corpus of literature, we find that these editorial interests lead on directly to the more elaborate patterns of interpretation employed later by Jews and Christians and which gave rise to a distinctive type of secondary literature with a methodology and techniques of interpretation peculiar to itself. If we are seeking to recover a genuine awareness of the theological meaning of prophecy, then we must surely be wholly committed to a historical understanding of how prophecy was appropriated as "the word of God," rather than to create for ourselves a rather artificial outline of the main ideological assumptions of the prophetic preaching. The counter argument that could be raised that, in the ways in which they interpreted prophecy, Jews and Christians have been very artificial and arbitrary, no doubt contains some truth. It has proved a difficult and demanding task to follow through the intricate web of verbal and literary artistry by means of which Jews and Christians have sought to hear in prophecy the word of God. Yet such processes are neither wholly unrestrained, nor yet wholly fanciful, but genuinely represent an attempt to find in prophecy a consistent and coherent message.

Before concluding this examination of some of the theological implications of the production of a body of prophetic literature in ancient Israel we may note what is probably its most startling and enduring consequence. This is the belief that a prophey could be delivered and await its fulfilment at an interval of several centuries after the time in which it had been given. So Matthew 1:22-3 could assert that the prophecy of the birth of the Immanuel child (Isa.7:14) could take place more than seven centuries after Isaiah's day, and without any attempt to understand the prophecy in the context of the circumstances in which it had originally been declared. Christianity has become wholly familiar with such an understanding of prophecy, although its roots go far back in the text of the Old Testament (cf. 1 Kings 13:32 and 2 Kings 23:17).[20] This expectation of a very prolonged interval between the giving of a prophecy and the time of its fulfillment must itself surely have been profoundly influenced, even if not actually originated, by the preservation of prophecies in writing. It no longer required living memory to retain a consciousness of the prophetic word that God had given, but its written preservation could ensure this. Moreover, as we have sought to emphasize in this study, the loss of the original context in which a prophetic saying had been spoken was replaced, once it was written down, by a new context of a literary nature. One type of context gave way to another with important consequences for the way in which the message was then to be understood.[21] More strikingly still, prophecies could be regarded as held in suspense, so that the time of their fulfillment could be regarded as not finally determined, or they could be regarded as susceptible of more than one fulfilment. I have argued elsewhere that it was an important feature of the New Testament's claim that prophecy had been fulfilled (i.e. "filled full") with the coming of Jesus Christ in order to regard Old Testament prophecy as completed and thereby closed off.[22] In any case the beliefs that written prophecy did so much to encourage-that fulfilment could take place after a centuries' long interval of time, or that a particular prophecy might have a multiplicity of fulfilments-inevitably had repercussions upon those aspects of prophecy which were felt to have greatest significance. Inevitably metaphors and verbal imagery of many kinds came to be recast and reinterpreted away from their original contexts to convey many meanings. Instead of the plain declarations of prophetic utterance, rooted in known events and related to known personalities, greater interest came to be attached to themes and imagery that could readily be applied and adapted to a variety of contexts. It is in this world that so much of the later Jewish and Christian apocalyptic imagery established its origins so that the dividing line between prophecy and apocalytpic becomes an increasingly blurred and indistinct one. In some measure the transition from prophecy to apocalyptic has provided for the theologian some exceedingly difficult and uncomfortable questions. Where religious meaning was at one time clear and unequivocal it seems to have become indistinct and many-faceted.[23] Yet we must contend that this same process was one which inevitably had its contrasting side. *Torah* and apocalyptic grew up together, so that eventually Christianity and Judaism responded in different ways to the inherent complexities and tensions of Jewish apocalyptic.

We may conclude, then, by arguing that the transition from oral to written prophecy had very far-reaching repercussions for the rise of a genuine theological understanding of the nature and activity of God. The claim of prophecy to present a message from the divine world about human affairs inevitably raised questios about the providential goals implicit in the divine will towards humankind. Once prophecy had come to be written down it became possible to formulate more elaborate and wide-ranging pictures of the nature of this divine activity, demanding of necessity more clearly defined descriptions of the nature and character of God. On the one hand, this encouraged intensely nationalistic and other worldly portrayals of God's ultimate purpose. Yet alongside these apocalyptic projections of the providential goal of history there was a need for a humane, relevant and more immediate, outline of what the God-humankind relantionship demanded. This found expression in a written *torah*, claiming itself to be a divinely revealed compendium of truth given through Moses. In this, something of the prophetic model of divine revelation has undoubtedly been powerfully influential. We may claim therefore that, in their different ways, both *torah* and apocalyptic owed much to the earlier manifestations of prophecy in ancient Israel. A marked turning point in the change from the older, more open, religion in which prophecy had played a major part to the later religion of a book was occasioned by the writing down of prophecy. This necessitated a deeper questioning of the nature and character of the One who was looked upon as the ultimate source and inspiration of all prophecy.

NOTES

1. This may be regarded as essentially the case at Mari where we possess letters referring to dream interpretations and prophetic revelations, but where no attempt was made to provide any comprehensive corpus of prophetic literature, or to provide a basis for comparing prophecies with each other. Cf. F.Ellemeier, *Prophetie in Mari und Israel*, Herzberg, 1968.

2. This becomes clear from the useful selection of viewpoints brought together by P.H.A. Neumann, *Das Prophetenverständnis in der Deutschsprachigen Forschung seit Heinrich Ewald*, Darmstadt, 1979. A fuller picture of Eichhorn's and Herder's work is to be found in E.Sehmsdorf, *Die Prophetenauslegung bei J.G.Eichhorn*, Göttingen, 1971.

3. So especially B.S.Childs, *Introduction to the Old Testament as Scripture*, London, 1979, pp.305ff. Cf. also J.Blenkinsopp, *Prophecy and Canon. A Contribution to the Study of Jewish Origins*, Notre Dame, 1977,pp.96ff.

4. Cf. J.J.Jackson (ed.). *Rhetorical Criticism. Essays in honor of James Muilenburg*

(Pittsburgh Theological Monograph Series 1), Pittsburgh, 1974, particularly the introduction by B.W.Anderson.

5. *Ezekiel 1-20* (Anchor Bible 22), Garden City, N.Y.,1983,pp18ff.

6. It is noteworthy that J.Vermeylen has argued that even the original Song of the Vineyard of Isaiah 5:1-7 should be regarded as a Deuteronomistic redactional composition. Cf. *Du prophète Isaïe a l'apocalyptique, Isaïe i-xxxv miroir d'un demi-milléenaire d'experience religieuse en Israel* (Études bibliques), Paris, 1977, Vol. 1, pp. 159ff. The majority of commentators have not taken such a view, but it nevertheless highlights the need to consider more fully the distinctions between oral and literary aspects of the prophetic tradition.

7. Cf. especially J.Goody, *The Domestication of the Savage Mind*, Cambridge, 1977, pp.36ff. A more literary perspective on the issues is discussed in W.J.Ong, *Orality and Literacy. The Technologizing of the Word*, London -New York, 1982.

8. W.J.Ong, "Writing Restructures Consciousness," *op.cit.*, pp. 78ff.

9. Cf. especially *Die Theologie der Propheten*, Bonn, 1875, and the somewhat modified position in his later work *Israels Propheten*, Tübingen, 1916, (2)1922.

10. *Old Testament Theology*, (Eng.Tr. D.Stalker) Vol.2, Edinburgh & London, 1965.

11. Cf. especially S.Mowinckel, *Prophecy and Tradition. The Prophetic Books in the Light of the Growth and History of the Tradition*, Olso, 1946; E.Nielsen, *Oral Tradition* (Studies in Biblical Theology 11), London, 1954, pp.39ff. Cf. W.J.Ong, *op.cit.*, pp.173f.:". . . biblical studies, like other textual studies, are inclined unwittingly to model the noetic and verbal economy of oral cultures on literacy, projecting oral memory as a variant of verbatim literate memory and thinking of what is preserved in oral tradition as a kind of text that is only waiting to be set down in writing."

12. Cf. S.Mowinckel, *Jesajas disiplene*, Oslo, 1926; J.Eaton, "The Origin of the Book of Isaiah", *VT* 9 (1959), pp.138-157, D.R.Jones, "The Tradition of the Oracles of Isaiah of Jerusalem", *ZAW* 67 (1955), pp.226-246. For Ezekiel reference must especially be made to W. Zimmerli, *Ezekiel*, 2 vols (Hermeneia Commentaries) Philadelphia, 1979, 1983, *passim;* also "Das Phänomen der 'Fortschreibung im Buche Ezechiel," *Prophecy. Fs. G. Fohrer* (BZAW150), Berlin - New York, 1980, pp.174-191.

13. This aspect of the material is strongly emphasised by R.P. Carroll. *From Chaos to Covenant. Uses of Prophecy in the Book of Jeremiah*, London, 1981, pp.151ff.

14. *Mündliche und schriftliche Tradition der vorexilischen Prophetbücher als Problem neueren Prophetenforschung* (FRLANT 73), Göttingen, 1979.

15. This may be maintained despite the important criticisms of the thesis concerning the Isaiah "Memoir" by O.Kaiser, *Isaiah 1-12*, 2nd ed., Eng Tr. by J.Bowden, London, 1983, pp.114ff.

16. The necessity for giving more scope in the interpretation of prophecy to the idea of fulfillment is argued in my essay "Prophecy and Fulfillment", *Epworth Review* 10 (1983), pp.72-82.

17. I am thinking here especially of the work by R.P.Carroll, *When Prophecy Failed: Reactions and Response to Failure in the Old Testament Prophetic Traditions*, London, 1979.

18. Cf. my essay, "Patterns in the Prophetic Canon," in G.W.Coats and B.O.Long (eds.) *Canon and Authority*, Philadelphia, 1977,pp.42-55.

19. The complexity of this subject is highlighted by E.Osswald, *Falsche Prophetie im Alten Testament*, Tübingen, 1962; J.A.Sanders "Hermenutics in True and False Prophecy", *Canon and Authority*, pp.21-41. Cf. also my treatment of the theme in *Prophecy and Tradition*, Oxford, 1975, pp.41-57.

20.   This point is brought out well by G. von Rad, *Studies in Deuteronomy* (Studies in Biblical Theology 9), London, 1947, pp.78-83.

21.   Cf. M. Fishbane, *Biblical Interpretation in Ancient Israel*, Oxford, 1985, pp.458ff.

22.   Cf. my essay, "Prophecy and Fulfillment," *Epworth Review* 10(1983), pp.72-82.

23.   This point is noted, rather inconclusively, by K.Koch, *The Prophets. Vol.2 The Babylonian and Persian Periods*, Eng Tr. M. Kohl, London, 1983, pp.188f.

Gerhard von Rad in American Dress
by Brevard S. Childs

There is a wide, international consensus that Gerhard von Rad developed a new theological paradigm by which to interpret the Old Testament. The roots of his understanding can be traced to his earliest works, but culminated in his epoch-making *Theologie des Alten Testaments* (I, 1957; II, 1960). The significance of his contribution is not to suggest that serious theological work had not long preceded him. Especially one recalls the magisterial Old Testament Theology of W. Eichrodt (1933-1939). Eichrodt treated certain topics so thoroughly, particularly in the field of the history of religion, that the next generation simply assumed his results. Although only a decade separated the age of these two scholars chronologically, such major disjunctions divided their approaches that it is necessary to assign them to different generations of Old Testament scholarship. Even in the choice of their debating partners one can discern the strikingly different concerns which stimulated their interests.

Many efforts have been made since von Rad's death in 1971 to assess his contribution to Old Testament studies.[1] The richness of his work is such that only a beginning has been made and undoubtedly major monographs on his work can be expected in the future. Certain emphases are obvious and strike even the casual reader. First, von Rad developed his theology around a newly developed understanding of the role of tradition history in closest conjunction with a sophisticated form critical approach to the literature. As is well known, Gunkel, Gressmann, Alt, and Mowinckel had previously turned from the preoccupation with the literary process of source analysis, and had pointed the way to the recovery of the depth dimension of the oral tradition. However, it was clearly von Rad who developed a means of exploiting this traditional dimension theologically, and thus introduced Gunkel and Alt to a new theological audience.[2]

Secondly, von Rad brought a remarkable degree of closeness to the biblical text, both in his commentaries and theology, which set him apart from his predecessors. His extreme sensitivity to the exact profile of the text resulted in his recovery of the rich, variegated diversity which resisted all efforts to designate an Old Testament center, or to systematize the tradition within overarching categories. However, his equal attention to the Old Testament as a whole with its developing lines of growth and transformation provided a major check against an atomization of the tradition into artificial trajectories.

Thirdly, von Rad as a conscious Christian theologian strove to do justice both to the original intention of an Old Testament author as well as to its subsequent hearing by the New Testament. In a 1952 article on Old Testament typology[3] he made a bold first attempt to develop a new critical understanding of an ancient Christian rendering of the Old Testament. His continual wrestling with the problem bore fruit in the final section of his theology (Vol.II, part 3) in which he saw the whole Old Testament history, in spite of its breaks and failures, culminating in the radically new redemptive event of Jesus Christ.

There is an additional element of uniqueness in von Rad's work which seems to me to lie close to the heart of his theology and which also accounts for his tremendous influence among Anglo-American readers. The issue has to do with his concerns for the "actualization" of ancient Old Testament traditions by a new generation of Israel. (*Vergegenwärtigung* is the term which he usually employs.) Von Rad sought to show that Israel's traditions did not remain a static deposit, but continued to reverberate in a living, dynamic manner. Thus, they not only retained their life, but provided the means by which the revelation of God continued to impinge upon the next generations. Although von Rad's primary concern focused on the descriptive level in showing how the need to actualize the tradition accounted for the on-going process of reworking older tradition by the layering of the material, he also recognized the homiletical significance of this process of representation for later Christian communities who sought to rediscover meaning for today's world from a past scriptural legacy.

In his dissertation *Actualization and Interpretation in Old Testament Prophecy* (Yale University, 1979), Joseph A. Groves was able to demonstrate that increasingly the concept of *Vergegenwärtigung* expanded in von Rad's thinking until it became the central category by which to encompass his major concerns. When von Rad wrote his important monograph in 1938, *Das formgeschichtliche Problem des Hexateuchs*, he reflected an initial ambiguity in relating cultic actualization with the literary process of the re-use of older tradition within a historical process. However, increasingly the separate strands of his thought—typology, promise and fulfillment, charismatic freedom— coalesced into one coherent vision of the Old Testament. In Volume I of his theology, actualization appears as a central hermeneutical force for the entire Old Testament. The requirement of faith was such that the tradition must also speak relevantly to the present, and actualization was deemed the process by which Israel realized its contemporaneity (pp.155ff.). In Volume II von Rad expanded the function of actualization even further. It was not merely a form of "poetic freedom" (p.105), but was one of Israel's "greatest achievements" (p.107). Actualization was a movement in which "the saving events were dissociated from the sphere of the cult and made available for the construction of a linear period of history"(p. 108).

The culmination of von Rad's work on actualization came in his attempt to relate the Old and New Testaments. The main thrust of his argument was that both testaments exhibit a similar use of tradition which is characterized by actualization. Just as the prophetic literature was marked by a fresh interpretation of the older tradition which is charismatic in nature, so this same freedom lies at the heart of the New Testament's use of the Old (Volume II, pp. 414ff.).

In sum, von Rad's understanding of actualization provided him with a hermeneutical means of resolving a host of persistent problems respecting the Old Testament. First, he was able to assign theological value to each stage in the lengthy process of historical development by treating the multilayered text as a witness to Israel's struggle to contemporize the past. Secondly, the continuing process allowed him to retain the diversity of the Old Testament within a broad theological movement from prophecy to fulfillment. Finally, the text's openness to the future provided an avenue for Christians to find a dynamic analogy for subsequent appropriation of an ancient legacy.

II

Although most of these elements of von Rad's theology have long been observed and evaluated, there remains another aspect of his thought which has not been adequately explored up to now, and provides the primary focus of this essay. The issue best emerges by focusing on the manner in which von Rad's theology has been appropriated in current American Old Testament scholarship, particularly in regard to his concept of actualization.

One does not have to look far in contemporary Old Testament writing to find a large group of American scholars whose work reflects the great attraction of von Rad. He is applauded for his ground-breaking form critical analysis, his exciting view of tradition history, and his theological sensitivity. However, above all he has been used as a warrant for a particular theological understanding of revelation and tradition which is characterized by its orientation toward the future, its creative flexibility, and its dynamic view of charisma. Von Rad is thought to offer major support for finding a theological analogy between Israel's handling of its past traditions and the modern task of reformulating our own past religious inheritance to suit the needs of a new age.

Douglas A. Knight[4] makes explicit reference to von Rad's concept of actualization (p.167) in developing his own understanding of revelation through tradition which seeks to avoid the emphasis on the Bible's objective, kerygmatic witness associated with Karl Barth and G.E. Wright. Rather, he assigns the human imagination a major role in establishing a parallel relationship between Yahweh's commitment and Israel's creativity (p.168).

Moreover, a consistent theme of James Sanders[5], Walter Brueggemann[6], and Paul Hanson[7] is that the modern interpreter stands in an analogous position to his own tradition as did Israel. The reader is constantly instructed that revelation does not depend upon a static text or on doctrines developed in the past. "...the great events of exodus, covenant, ... exile, second exodus, and the life of Christ did not constitute the 'frozen' scenario of a primordial myth, but were unique historical events which set in motion a creative ... process."[8] The modern church participates in the same "traditioning process" and also employs the same freedom, openness to the future, and flexibility which Israel is alleged to have possessed.

Of course, there are variations of emphasis within this same overarching theological construal. Sanders uses the term "canon" to designate a continuing process, oscillating between poles of stability and adaptibility, by which both Israel and the modern church seek to open up ancient texts for new contemporary situations. There is never a fixed canonical context, but an endless search for authentic identity. The Bible contains "unrecorded hermeneutics"[9] which, when critically recovered, offer axioms for modern application. There are also certain discernible moral guidelines which indicate God's abiding interest in the oppressed, in human liberation, and in an egalitarian society.

Hanson's interpretation of revelation according to a model of "Dynamic Transcendence" also reflects influence from von Rad, but in a form mediated by G.E. Wright. However, the terminology of both scholars has been radically secularized by Hanson. *Heilsgeschichte* has become a "purposeful movement through time and space."[10] Transcendence develops within a polarity between visionary and pragmatic tendencies of history. Two trajectories represented by a cosmic and a teleological vector constitute an essential dynamic of this developing reality which moves through time. Confessional heritage and contemporary experience are related in a dialectical process of criticism and renewal. Proper exercise of this hermeneutic allegedly protects the Bible from becoming an "archaic relic" (p. 17), but enables the contemporary believer to participate in creative living and self-transcending service.

It is obvious that within such a theological framework the traditional doctrine of the Bible as a corpus of authoritative writings must be seriously revised. Robert Laurin[11] expresses this common theology succinctly: ". . . canonization was an unfortunate freezing of tradition growth. Canonization was untrue to tradition history and its contemporizing process" (p. 271). Laurin then proceeds to draw the logical Christological implications from his position: "No stage, not even the New Testament, is the final or more authoritative stage. The people of God in every generation must engage in the canonizing process" (p. 272). In sum, there is no privileged time within the divine will, there are no special witnesses, there is no unique divine manifestation. Rather, these have been replaced by traditioning process, dynamic transcendence, and monotheistic pluralism!

III

How does one assess this peculiar American theological appropriation of von Rad? Is it a move which stands in continuity with von Rad's own goals or is it a strange aberration which should be rejected out of hand? For a variety of reasons the answers to these questions are not obvious or immediately apparent, but require further exploration.

The first point to make is that recognition of the very different historical context in which von Rad wrote would caution against any hastily drawn conclusions. In striking contrast to the American scholars who all reflect influences from the turbulent sixties and the post-Vietnam era, von Rad started his theological training under the deepening shadow of National Socialism, but also in the period of the rebirth of confessional theology in the 1920's. He then experienced the defeat of Germany and the tensions of rebuilding a divided nation after the debacle. The issues which he faced were of a very different order from the next generation of his students. Specifically in terms of the Old Testament discipline, he was constantly doing battle against German Liberal Protestantism and an anti-Semitic German nationalism which sought to relegate the Old Testament to oblivion. In addition, much of his energy was focused on overcoming the atomization of the Old Testament through a sterile form of literary and historical study. He struggled with Herder, Gunkel, and Alt to find a means of using rigorous historical criticism to recover a living and holistic understanding of Israel's tradition.

A variety of theological issues were of highest priority for him. In his early writings one can detect influences from dialectical theology, but more in terms of the charged atmosphere of that era rather than from a direct influence of Barth.[12] His major theological education stemmed from classic Lutheran dogmatics, and also from his wide knowledge of German romantic literature. Throughout his life von Rad continued to wrestle with the 19th century "Erlangen theology." Although he was very critical of J.C.K. von Hofmann's organic concept of Heilsgeschichte,[13] nevertheless he succeeded in reformulating many of Hofmann's central ideas for a post-Wellhausen age. Von Rad strongly resisted the so-called Christological exegesis of Wilhelm Vischer in the 1930's[14] which he thought offered an unfortunate temptation to the church. He argued that Vischer sacrificed the diversity of the Old Testament by hearing only one note. Thus he lost the dynamic movement of promise and fulfillment.

Late in his career von Rad wrote a heated response to Conzelmann[15] who had attacked him by developing Bultmann's thesis that the Old Testament's role was solely that of "miscarriage." Von Rad used the occasion to reject all forms of historicism and to plead for a far broader view of historical knowledge. Already on an earlier occasion he had made reference to Gadamer's position[16] which he used to refute attacks from those who alleged that he disregarded historical "facts."

In spite of these various fronts to which von Rad directed his attention, certain fundamental lines emerge from all his writings which, in my judgment, have not been correctly heard by those in America who have aligned themselves with certain elements of his theology. Above all, there is a Christological center to von Rad's exegesis. Certainly it is not in the traditional allegorical mode, nor along the lines formulated by Vischer, but nevertheless an approach to the Old Testament which is profoundly Christian. He writes: "We receive the Old Testament from the hands of Jesus Christ, and therefore all exegesis of the Old Testament depends on whom one thinks Jesus Christ to be."[17] Or again, ". . . for Christians the Old Testament only has meaning in so far as it refers to Christ and was able to speak in the light of Christ" (Vol.II, p.332).

Von Rad continued to express amazement at how the New Testament took over the Old Testament—its narratives, prayers, and prophecies. He argued that this could not have occurred if the Old Testament were an alien religion lacking a fundamental compatibility. "This could not have happened if the Old Testament writings had not themselves contained pointers to Christ and had been hermeneutically adapted to such a merger" (Vol.II, p.33). The union was possible because of a radical transformation of the Old Testament material in the light of the new saving event inaugurated by Christ. The New Testament writers used an astonishing charismatic freedom of interpretation by which to see everything in the Old Testament as referring to Christ (Vol.II, p.329). There was never any one fixed method of actualization, but an incredible freedom reclaiming the old traditions as witnesses to Jesus Christ.

Von Rad never wearied of stressing that the "Old Testament can only be read as a book in which expectation keeps mounting up to vast proportions" (Vol.II, p.321). The New Testament brings to an end the process initiated by the Old and is its "final reinterpretation" (vol.II, p.321). Or again, "Israel's history with God thrusts forward violently into the future, and in the New Testament. . . it reaches its *last* hermeneutical modification and its *full* and *final* interpretation" (Vol.II, p.332, italics mine).

Von Rad's concern with the traditioning process and his demand for flexible, dynamic interpretation relates directly to his Christological concern to do justice to the full dimensions of God's revelation in Jesus Christ. Indeed, Jesus Christ is not imprisoned within a book nor related to the historical past. As God's new eschatological event the Christian Church shares with Israel the role of living between promise and fulfillment and anticipates a continued renewal of God's spirit. Von Rad shows no interest in a philosophy of world history or a theology of process. Jesus Christ has brought to a full completion God's saving events. Therefore, when American Old Testament scholars reject the confession of the finality of Jesus Christ in claiming that no stage in world history is definitive in an on-going process of human development (cf.

Laurin, *op.cit.*), they are moving in a direction which is basically antithetical to von Rad's theology. No sharper contrast between von Rad and his appropriators can be imagined than in Paul Hanson's diagram of redemptive history in which the coming of Jesus Christ is registered in a diagram as a minor offshoot in a historical stream comparable to the desecration of the Second Temple under the Seleucids![18]

In spite of the clarity with which von Rad has expressed the Christological center of his interpretation of the Old Testament, a word of caution is still called for. Von Rad was far too complex a theologian for any simple formulation of his position. In all fairness, one must admit that other notes occasionally sound in his writings which offer at least some basis for construing—rather, misconstruing—his theology after the manner of American Protestant liberalism. At times he spoke approvingly of the slogan of the "radical openness of history to the future," but modified it immediately as a future to be released by God (Vol.II, p.361). Moreover, in his essay "The Preaching of Deuteronomy and our Preaching"[19] von Rad suggested an important analogy between the preaching of Deuteronomy and modern proclamation. As in the past, the modern proclaimer of God's word needs both courage and freedom to address an old word into a new situation. Von Rad's examples are loosely enough drawn to allow much freedom in developing the exact nature of the analogy.

Finally, von Rad ends his discussion of the law according to the New Testament with the statement: "There is in fact no normative interpretation of the Old Testament. Every age has the task of hearing what the old book has to say to it in the light of its own insights and its own needs. Any age which loses this charismatic approach will find no help from either Paul or Matthew or the Apostle to the Hebrews" (Vol.II, p.409). If this statement is read in the context of von Rad's larger interpretation of the charismatic relation between the testaments, it is thoroughly consistent with his Christology. However, if taken by itself, it can be heard as allowing each new generation freedom to interpret the Old Testament according to its own needs and experience apart from any normative role exercised by the coming of Jesus Christ.

IV

It can, of course, be argued that von Rad's formulations have been at times imprecise and that little importance should be attached to their misconstrual. In my opinion, the issue lies deeper than this approach to von Rad's theology would suggest. Moreover, it is confirmed by the extent to which von Rad has been accommodated to the ideology of American theological liberalism. I would argue the case that there is a flaw in von Rad's theology which has functioned both in American, British, and European theology to blur the Christological center of his theology. The issue turns on his concept of the role of the Old Testament canon. In Volume II, (p.328), he addressed the objection that the taking over of the Old Testament material into the New Testament does not share a comparable process since the Old Testament had already been fixed in writing as Sacred Scripture. He responded that the difference is not a radical one and really affects only the formal side of actualization. In my opinion, most New Testament scholars would disagree with von Rad's assessment. Rather, a new dynamic of interpretation was unleashed by the textualization of the tradition. Certainly from the formal side many of the means by which the New Testament appropriated the Old are seen to stand in closest proximity with both Qumran and rabbinic Judaism. However, also in terms of content the New Testament writers along with other Hellenistic groups read the Old Testament as a collection of inspired writings and not as free-floating traditions.

The element which set apart the New Testament from the various forms of Judaism was the content of its Christology. Clearly von Rad would agree. However, the essential point to make in addition is that the formation of a Christian canon of Scripture was also a derivative of Christology. An authoritative collection of sacred writings, consisting of the witness of the prophets and apostles, bore testimony to the unique revelation of God in Jesus Christ both in its promised and fulfilled forms. The canonical writings were set apart as special, and to be distinguished from later ecclesiastical tradition, because they alone testified to the unique entry into history of the incarnated Christ.

In my opnion, von Rad was mistaken in his judging that the formation of the canon was of minor exegetical and theological importance. As a result, I think that his description of the ways in which the New Testament relates to the Old Testament needs an important corrective. Nevertheless, von Rad was able to develop his Old Testament theology firmly according to a Christological goal, which would tolerate no Old Testament center apart from the New. However, his omission of the Christological role of the Christian canon has had the effect that a new generation of Old Testament scholars can now find a warrant in his Old Testament theology for a process of human development which operates apart from the decisive revelation of Jesus Christ, who is God's final and authoritative word to the world.

Footnotes

1. W.H. Schmidt, "'*Theologie des Alten Testaments*' *vor und nach Gerhad von Rad*," *Verkündigung und Forschung, EvThBeih* 17, 1972, pp.1-25; *Gerhard von Rad. Seine Bedeutung für die Theologie. Drei Reden von H.W. Wolff, R. Rendtorff, W. Pannenberg* (Munich 1973); James L. Crenshaw, *Gerhard von Rad* (Waco, Tx. 1978).

2. W. Baumgartner's review of H. -J. Kraus' book, *Geschichte der historisch-kritischen Erforschung des Alten Testaments*, 1956 (*ThR* NF 25, 1959, pp.93ff.), criticized the author for incorporating Gunkel too firmly within modern theological concerns.

3. "*Typologische Auslegung des Alten Testaments*", *EvTh* 12, 1952, pp.17-33; reprinted *GSAT* II (Munich 1973), pp.272-288.

4. "Revelation through Tradition", *Tradition and Theology in the Old Testament*, ed. D.A. Knight, (Philadelphia 1977,) *pp.143-180.*

5. "Hermeneutics", *IDB Suppl.*, pp. 402-407; *Canon and Community*, (Philadelphia: Fortress, 1984), pp. 28ff.

6. *The Creative Word*, (Philadelphia:1982), pp.lff.

7. *Dynamic Transcendence*, Philadephia:1978), pp. 64ff.

8. *Dynamic Transcendence*, p.62.

9. *Canon and Community*, p.46.

10. *Dynamic Transcendence*, p.14.

11. "Tradition and Canon," *Tradition and Theology in the Old Testament*, ed., D.A. Knight, pp.261-274.

12. In his dissertation, *Das Gottesvolk im Deuteronomium (BWANT 47)*, Stuttgart 1929, such existentialist phrases as *hic et nunc*, etc. appear.

13. *Old Testament Theology*, volume II, pp.362.

14. "*Das Christuszeugnis des Alten Testaments. Eine Auseinandersetzung mit Wilhelm Vischers gleichnamigen Buch*", *ThBl* 14, 1935, pp.249-254.

15. "*Antwort auf Conzelmanns Fragen*," *EvTh* 24, 1964, pp.388-394.

16. "*Offene Fragen im Umkreis einer Theologie des Alten Testaments*," *GSAT* II, Munich 1973, p.299.

17. *Genesis*,ET, rev. ed. (Philadelphia 1973), p.43.

18. *Dynamic Transcendence*, p.55.

19. *Interpretation* 15, 1961, pp.3-13.

Proverbs and Theological Exegesis
by Roland E. Murphy. O. Carm.

The Book of Proverbs would seem to be a very modest candidate for theological exegesis. It certainly does not contribute directly to studies in biblical theology, if it is even mentioned by them. Yet, "exegesis as a theological discipline," as James L. Mays has phrased it, issues a distinctive challenge: Why should Proverbs be tacitly, as it were, decanonized?[1]

There are obvious reasons for the neglect of this book. Biblical wisdom has been recognized particularly in this century as an international phenomenon. The effect has been to reduce Proverbs to the level of Ptahhotep or Amenemope, with which it can certainly be compared. There is an ironic edge to such a comparison. It might conceivably have oriented research toward a biblical basis for the understanding of the theological dimension of international wisdom. Instead, scholarship has allowed it to water down the biblical counterpart to universal human experience, and merely to tolerate the Book of Proverbs. Secondly, the book itself is caught up in a biblical dialectic with Job and Ecclesiastes, which has modified the optimistic world view which undergirds the book—so much so that scholars have spoken of the bankruptcy of proverbial wisdom.[2] This point, however, may not be as strong as it seems in view of the continuation of the wisdom tradition in Sirach and the Wisdom of Solomon. Evidently the community that retained Proverbs in the canon did not see it as bankrupt.

Thirdly, if one assumes that biblical theology has to be centered on an entity called Yahwism, which is defined by the patriarchal promises, the Exodus experience and Sinai covenant, then Proverbs is outside the pale, hardly on the "margin" of biblical belief. Many scholars would counter that the "Yahweh-sayings" in the book are the ingredient that saves it for biblical theology.[3] But is this not shortsighted? If Yahwism and wisdom are so thoroughly divorced as is implied in this assumption, the band-aid exegesis which trades on the sacred name will not save the Book of Proverbs. This issue raises the possibility of a deeper level of understanding the wisdom phenomenon—it is not to be understood in the light of the assumptions of the Yahwist/wisdom dichotomy.[4]

Fourthly, history bears out the "benign neglect" of Proverbs.

No history of the exegesis of the book has ever emerged, but one gets the impression from certain bench marks that it has served as little more than an "enforcer" for moral guidance. Only fragments of the pertinent works of the Greek and Latin Fathers have been preserved.[5] In the medieval period, the fancy of Bede and Albert the Great was caught by the 'eset hayil of 31:10-31. It is an intriguing fact that Melanchthon wrote more than one commentary on Proverbs, as busy as he was in the hectic days of the Reformation. He apparently considered the book important.[6] But the tendency up into modern times has been to relegate the book somewhere behind the Torah as contributing to the ethical ideals of Israel. It may be noted that the recent and worthy commentary of O. Plöger declines to follow the customary format of the BKAT series in which his work appears. The "Ziel," or "goal," which was designed to emphasize the theological edge of a book in this series, is provided for chapters 1-9, but it is abandoned in chapters 10-31.[7]

In view of all this it is surely hazardous to speak of the theological exegesis of the Book of Proverbs! But there is no escape from this issue, as anyone who teaches in a seminary knows. There is the inevitable question raised concerning the theological relevance of this book. What can be said? I will attempt an answer from two points of view, suggested by the presentation of wisdom in the Book of Proverbs, both as sayings which capture experience and as Lady Wisdom, a mysterious divine personification.

The Wisdom Experience

There are certain presuppositions undergirding the claims that are gathered up in the phrase, "wisdom experience," and these should be explicitly stated.

1. Wisdom theology is creation theology. This well known dictum of W. Zimmerli has been widely accepted.[8] Zimmerli's purpose was to discover the proper niche for wisdom within the framework of Old Testament theology, and he explicated this in terms of creation, specifically Genesis 1:28 (the divine mandate to humans as to their relationship to the earth and all living things). His insight opens up a new perspective on Proverbs. The book is more than collections of sayings. These are inspired by a whole experience of the created world (and God). Wisdom is more than well-turned nuggets of human observation; it is an attitude toward creation and life.

2. God (in the case of Israelite wisdom, this must be YHWH) reveals himself in human experiences. This is the meaning of the

striking statement of G. von Rad: "Israel knew nothing of the aporia which we read into these proverbs. It was perhaps her greatness that she did not keep faith and knowledge apart. The experiences of the world were for her always divine experiences as well, and the experiences of God were for her experiences of the world."[9]

There may be other presuppositions, but these two are fundamental for a description of the wisdom experience.

By wisdom experience I mean the experience which generated the insights into the world and human beings (from which in the Israelite view God is never absent), the mĕšālîm that resulted from the outlay of energy and enterprise with which Israel grappled with the mysteries of creation and daily existence. The wisdom experience consists in the encounter, which is encoded in the proverbs. Both sayings and admonitions reflect the experience and the attempt to communicate it. The experience itself is multifaceted. It can begin, as Aristotle (*Metaphysics*, I, ii, 9) remarked about philosophy, in wonder (*thaumadzein*). Thus an encounter with the mystery of the other in sexual attraction leads to a comparison with other "ways" (*derek*) in the world, such as the way of an eagle in the air (Prov. 30:18-20). On the other hand, an event as modest as the summer storing of food by ants has something to say about wisdom and smallness. The emotional levels of human reactions do not go unnoticed. They are reflected in normal conditions (the effect of joy upon a person, Prov.13:12, 14:10, 17:22), as well as in conflicting feelings (sadness in laughter, Prov.14:13). An important emphasis is self-control, most sharply expressed in the many sayings relative to speech.[10] If one can control this aspect of conduct, then the possibility of "hearing," or docility, presents itself.

An essential ingredient in the wisdom experience is the ability to listen. Solomon asked for a "listening heart" as the gift by which he might govern the people of God (I Kings 3:9). Already the Egyptian sages had insisted upon "hearing"; Ptahhotep in his Epilogue mentions the ideal of a "master-hearer." The fool is precisely the one who will not listen, who lacks a sense of docility. The *tōkaḥat*, or "reproof," occurs about a dozen times in Proverbs; it is something to be heard and loved, for it leads to correction and improvement. "The reproofs of discipline are a way to life" (Prov. 6:23). One who is wise in one's eyes (*i.e.* does not listen to advice; Prov. 12:15), is in the greatest danger; then there is more hope for a fool than for such a person (Prov. 26:12). This basic attitude underscores an openness of character, a readiness to change and improve.

The wisdom experience is not only meant to be constitutive of a person's life; at the same time it is destined to lead one to life, a fuller life. The wise do not remain stagnant, but move into the swim of life with observations to capture successive events. These are not randomly perceived, but coordinated towards the kerygma of the sage: the good life. Finding a way to live, to cope with the mysterious events of everyday experience—this is the goal of the wise person. The motivation of the good life sounds more cold and calculating than it is. The sages were aware of anomalies in everyday existence. One might be poor because of laziness (Prov. 25:30-34), but poverty was not always explicable, and it had to be addressed with the solicitude characteristic of Israel's ethos (Prov. 14:31). There existed many areas of life that were not amenable to the "steering" (*tahbulôt;* Prov. 1:5) capabilities of the sage. It would be a mistake for the modern reader to fail to hear the uncertainties and mysteries in the midst of so much forthrightness and confidence as the Book of Proverbs exudes. In that book of collections are acknowledgments such as 3:11-12 (the discipline of the Lord as a sign of divine favor), and the awesome admissions of Agur (Prov. 30:1-3); no "easy rider" he!

Finally, the wisdom experience, like wisdom itself, is inconceivable without "fear of God/Lord."[11] Despite the sometimes frantic urging of the sage, wisdom itself is not simply there for the taking (or "hearing"). It is a divine *gift* (Prov. 2:6; cf. Sirach, 43:33; 51:13-14; Wisdom of Solomon, 7:7; 9:4). It is rooted in fear of the Lord:

The fear of the Lord is the beginning of knowledge:
wisdom and instruction fools despise (Prov. 1:17).
The beginning of wisdom is the fear of the Lord, and
knowledge of the Holy One is understanding (Prov. 9:10).

These sayings mean that the fear of the Lord leads to wisdom. It is the indispensable prerequisite. This is an extraordinary claim, for it sets out the fundamental orientation of the wisdom enterprise. The wisdom experience derives from a basic attitude towards divinity, towards the numen.

However, one may ask if all this is theology. There is a tendency in biblical scholarship to recognize a theological level only where there is an explicit mention of God, and in the case of biblical wisdom, the sacred name. Only then, it is presumed, can one speak of Israelite religious wisdom. I would submit that this is not necessary, and one should not be guided by the categories of religious and secular which we impose according to our particular judgment. Israel considered its experience, and ultimately its wisdom, to be theological because it bears on various aspects of the human condition *sub specie creationis vel creatoris.*

There is a "theology" of Proverbs, but it is not the speculative analysis with which we tend to identify modern theology. Knowledge is rather being in and doing the truth. It might be more exactly described as "theological anthropology" in the words of the late Karl Rahner. This means that it is an understanding of humans in terms of their basic relatedness to divinity. It is not exhaustive; in fact it was accompanied by Israel's reaction to God's journey with her through history. But it captures an essential dimension of reality: the experience of God in the world. This is not the place to attempt a correlation between Proverbs and the theology of Rahner, but the following description of Rahner's work may suffice: "The God experienced in this 'mysticism of everyday things' is not the distilled essence of things, not the highest abstraction from the world, but the experience of God's life at the very heart of the world, in flesh, in time and in history. Perhaps the greatest dualism that Karl Rahner overcame is that between God and the world. For him they are never identical, but neither are they ever separate, so that God and the world are experienced and known together. Presence to self, presence to world and presence to God are all aspects of one and the same experience, the experience of God's real presence in the world which he created to be his real symbol."[12]

Moreover, this "theological anthropology" does not consist merely in the sayings and admonitions, as if they constituted an immutable standard for human conduct, or a complete program for living. The very dialectic within the wisdom movement (Qohelet's modification of wisdom) points to the value of the "wisdom experience" which lies behind it. It is this experience which is the model for living, as much as the individual *mĕšālîm.* Here biblical theology is not frozen into a text, but into the reality that lies behind the text. The total meaning comes from the experience and its literary encoding. By its nature, this is tentative, open, always "listening." The Bible provides a mandate for this style of living, which remains open-ended in its task of coping with life.

Lady Wisdom

The Book of Proverbs is filled with antitheses: the wise person and the fool, the righteous and the wicked, etc. The same style of contrast exists betwen Lady Wisdom and Dame Folly (Prov. 9). But there is probably no greater antithesis within Proverbs than between the practical sayings which dominate the book and Lady Wisdom. How is one to put together the earthy, everyday wisdom of the sayings with the majestic figure who appears with divine authority in chapters 1-9, especially 1, 8, and 9? The sayings rest on the authority of tradition, the mirror of experience, and the persuasiveness of the sage. The authority of Lady Wisdom is no less than herself: the one who gains her gains life, and the one who misses, is dead (Prov. 8:35-36). Who is this Lady, and how does she function in a theological exegesis of the book? Perhaps there are several answers to both of these questions.

Modern scholarship has been more inclined to speculate on the origins of this figure than to present an identification. The most recent study by B. Lang rehearses the various solutions.[13] Many models have been proposed: Canaanite Ashtarte, Egyptian Maat, Mesopotamian Inanna, the "Wisdom" of the unsteady text of Ahiqar (lines 94-95), and Isis (as influencing Sirach 24). These comparisons are of unequal value, and none has established itself. Even were one to admit the highly probable influence of Egyptian *ma'at* upon the description of Wisdom in Proverbs 1-9, very little has been done towards the interpretation of the figure itself.[14] Wisdom is clearly not a person, a deity, such as *ma'at* came to be in Egyptian religion. Indeed it seems wiser to avoid the term "hypostasis," which has been defined in diverse manners, and deal with "personification," a literary procedure.[15] This personification is without doubt the most striking in the Bible; there is nothing else like it.

The identity of Lady Wisdom emerges from the description which she gives of herself in Proverb 8. Of primary importance is her origin from the Lord before creation (8:22ff.). Whether she is possessed, created, or begotten (v. 22, *qānānî*), she is certainly born of God. There is a repeated emphasis on her origin *before* creation. This prerogative is important for she knows all about the creation which she has witnessed (as in Job 38:21 — he would have known, had he been born before the creation of light and darkness). Her actual participation in the work of creation seems likely (cf. Prov. 3:19), but the problem of the meaning of *'āmôn* (crafts[wo]man? nursling?) in verse 30 prevents certainty. The second characteristic is that she is all delight, playing on the surface of the earth, and finding delight in human beings. This outreach of Wisdom to humanity is particularly striking. Sirach is going to develop the theme at great length, and he interprets Wisdom's "dwelling in Jacob" to be the gift of the Torah, or Law (Sir.24:8,23). But what does this prerogative mean within the Book of Proverbs? G. von Rad advanced the stimulating view that Wisdom is the "self-revelation of creation," not a divine attribute, but "that mysterious attribute, by virtue of which she [creation, or the world] turns towards men to give order to their lives."[16] I have argued that von Rad did not go far enough; rather, Lady Wisdom is the Lord's self-revelation through creation.[17] In view of Ben Sira's later identification of wisdom with Torah, perhaps one should not be too apodictic about identification. But even here the comparison with Ben Sira suggests that the solution to the problem of identity rests basically with divine origin. "All wisdom comes from the Lord. . . . He has poured her forth upon all his works" (Sir.1:1-9). The figure of Lady Wisdom is thus open-ended, flexible, as Ben Sira has shown. But within the Book of Proverbs she is the divine summons issued to Israel through creation to heed the lessons of the wisdom experience.[18]

It does not seem possible really to explain why Wisdom is personified as a woman. The obvious reasons are inadequate. Little is to be learned from the fact that ḥokmāh is a feminine noun, or that there are many female personifications in the Bible ("Daughter Zion," etc.). It is true that the main pitch of the sages (were they all male, as so many presume?) is to the education of males ("my son," so frequent in Prov. 1-9). By focusing on *Lady* Wisdom, the plea could be made quite strong, with an erotic touch: "Say to Wisdom, 'You are my sister!'" (Prov. 7:4). Gender clearly functions in the development of the presentation, but it is not the dominant factor. On the other hand, how is one to account for the extraordinary emphasis on the avoidance of the "strange woman" (zārāh, nokriyyāh) and the adulteress in Proverbs 2:16-19; 5:1-20; 6:20-35; 7:6-27? Even here there may be lurking an overlay of Israel's dark past, the danger of the fertility rites, but now drawn into a contrast with true fidelity. However, this is speculation.

While Lady Wisdom's origin is obscure, her function is explicit, and it is one: to offer life (cf. Deut.30:15-19). She serves as a prophet who condemns fools and calls the simple to attention to her message (Prov. 1:20-31). In Chapter 8, even in the grandeur of all her self-description, her appeal remains the same: "So now, O children, listen to me. . . the one who finds me finds life. . . (8:32-35). In

Chapter 9, she appears as one who issues an invitation to a meal, and the same issue of life and death is continued. Participation in her banquet means life (9:6), while the guests of Dame Folly end up in Sheol (9:18).

By means of this personification, the Book of Proverbs has provided *the* motivation for wise conduct. All the customary one-line motivations in the admonitions pale into insignificance before the imperious claims of Herself. She guarantees the success of the wisdom experience.

FOOTNOTES

1. *Exegesis as a Theological Discipline*, Inaugural Address delivered April 20, 1960, in Schauffler hall, Union Theological Seminary, Richmond. Certain passages by Professor Mays deserve to be singled out as pertinent to the purpose of this article:
The exegete "may concern himself with grammar, dates, literary forms, parallels with other cultural and religious phenomena. But will he do all this for the sake of knowing what the text itself means to say, for what reason, and to whom? Will he accept the text's own self-understanding as decisive? Only an affirmative answer will enable the historical exegete really to interpret his text" (p.20).
"The concepts and categories and concerns which an exegete brings to a biblical passage are the indispensable prerequisites for the occurrence of understanding, the apprehension of meaning. Without them there would simply be no contact between the words of the passage and the mind of the interpreter. . . . The problem with presuppositions is not that we should have them, but whether we are aware of them, can formulate them cogently, are willing and ready to test them in the functional process of interpretation" (p.23).
The present writer recalls with gratitude the challenging theological discussions which marked the annual meetings (1959-1965) of *Interpretation*'s editorial council under the leadership of James Mays, and is happy to dedicate this article to him.

2. Cf. R. E. Murphy, "Qohelet's 'Quarrel' with the Fathers," in *From Faith to Faith. Essays in Honor of Donald G. Miller*, ed. D. Y. Hadidian (PTMS 31; Pittsburgh: Pickwick Press, 1979) pp.235-245. G. L. Sheppard has pointed out the manner in which Qohelet was received by a later generation (time of Sirach): "The Epilogue to Qohelet as Theological Commentary," *CBQ* 39 (1977), pp. 182-189.

3. See R. N. Whybray, "Yahweh-sayings and their Contexts in Proverbs, 10, 1-22, 16," *La Sagesse de l'Ancien Testament*, ed. M. Gilbert (BETL 51; Leuven: University Press, 1979), pp.153-165.

4. See the thoughtful article of John J. Collins, "Proverbial Wisdom and the Yahwist Vision," *Gnomic Wisdom*, ed. J. D. Crossan (Semeia 17; Chico: Scholars Press, 1980) pp.1-17. He relates Yahwism and wisdom by way of style, not content: "similar thought patterns were at work in both historical and sapiential traditions" (p. 14).

5. For the importance of Proverbs 8 in the Arian controversy, see the references in A. Grillmeier, *Christ in Christian Tradition* (2nd ed.; Atlanta, John Knox, 1975) Volume I, p. 591, and especially M. Simonetti, "Sull interpretazione patristicadi Proverbi 8,22," *Studi sull' Arianesimo* (Rome, 1965, pp. 9-87; the latter was not available to me.

6. Cf. H. Sick, *Melanchthon als Ausleger des Alten Testaments* (BGBH 2; Tübingen: Mohr/Siebeck, 1959) *pp. 4-6;* the influence of Reformation categories made itself felt, and by 1555 he understood the Torah and proverbs as valid for those who are justified by

faith; these books teach them about good works which please God (p. 38). A brief summary of the interpretation of the Book of Proverbs from Nicholas of Lyra to modern times is given in B. Lang, *Die weisheitliche Lehrrede* (SB 54; Stuttgart: KBW, 1972) pp. 11-26.

7. CF. O. Plöger, *Sprüche Salomos (Proverbia)* (BKAT 17; Neukirchen-Vluyn: Neukirchener, 1984).

8. W. Zimmerli, "The Place and Limit of the Wisdom on the Framework of the Old Testament Theology," *Studies in Ancient Israelite Wisdom,* ed. J. Crenshaw (New York: Ktav, 1976), pp. 314-326.

9. *Wisdom in Israel* (Nashville, 1972), p. 62.

10. Cf. W. Buhlmann, *Von rechten Reden und Schweigen* (OBO 12; Freiburg: Universitatsverlag, 1976). He deals with the sayings in chapters 10:1-22:16 and 25:1-9:27, limiting himself to only positive (as opposed to lies, etc.) speech, with over seventy examples.

11. See the discussion of fear of the Lord in R. E. Murphy, "Religious Dimensions of Israelite Wisdom," in the Frank M. Cross Festschrift (forthcoming).

12. Cf. W. Dych, "The Achievement of Karl Rahner," *TD* 31 (1984), pp.325-33; the quotation is from page 332.

13. Cf. *Frau Weisheit* (Düsseldorf: Patmos, 1975), pp.147-176. His own solution is that Lady Wisdom is personified school wisdom (pp.168-170).

14. The best treatment of this issue is C. Kayatz, *Studien zu Proverbien 1-9* (WMANT 22; Neukirchen-Vluyn, Neukirchener, 1966); see also O. Keel, *Die Weisheit spielt vor Gott* (Freiburg: Universitätsverlag, 1974).

15. See the judicious remarks on this topic by R. Marcus, "On Biblical Hypostases of Wisdom," *HUCA* 23/I (1950-51), pp.157-171.

16. *Op. cit.*, pp.144-176, esp. 151.

17. Cf. "Wisdom and Creation," *JBL* 104 (1985), pp.3-11.

18. Cf. R. E. Murphy, "The Faces of Wisdom in the Book of Proverbs," *Mélanges bibliques et orientaux en l'honneur de M. H. Cazelles*, ed. A. Caquot et M. Delcor (AOAT 212; Neukirchen-Vluyn: Neukirchener, 1981), pp.337-345.

Female Language for God:
Should the Church Adopt it?

By Elizabeth Achtemeier

It is a pleasure to participate in this <u>Festschrift</u>, honoring James L. Mays on his sixty-fifth birthday. One of the hermeneutical areas on which he has commented in recent years has been the feminist interpretation of the Scriptures, and it is with a specific aspect of that interpretation, namely, with the use of female language for God, that I would like to deal.

There is no doubt whatsoever that the church's continuing discrimination against women is a scandal to the gospel of Jesus Christ. The Christian faith proclaims that both male and female are made in the image of God (Gen. 1:27), that husband and wife are to join flesh in a marital union of mutual helpfulness (Gen. 2:18), that the ancient enmity between the sexes and the subordination of women are a result of human sin (Gen. 3), that that sinful enmity and subordination have been overcome by the death and resurrection of Jesus Christ (Gal. 3:28), and that all women and men alike are called to equal discipleship in the service of their risen Lord. The Scriptures further show that many of the early New Testament church communities placed no restrictions on the functions of women in their exercise of that discipleship, as so many recent studies have pointed out.[1] The Christian gospel is a gospel of freedom and service, in Christ, for male and female alike, as countless faithful women and men have discovered down through the history of the church. For the modern church, therefore, to deny women ordination, or leadership roles, or influence and status and participation in the life of the Body of Christ equal to those of males, simply on the basis of women's biology, is a denial of that freedom with which Christ has set us free and slavery once again to sin and the world. Having been given new life in Christ, women justly cry out against such discrimination:

> Oh, you cannot imagine what it is to love the new age with all one's heart and soul, yet to be bound hand and foot, chained to the laws and customs of our country.[2]

In reaction to such discrimination, some women have left the church in deep anger and now condemn its Scriptures and faith. Others have decided *a priori* that its message holds nothing for them and have turned to non-Judaic, non-Christian, or pagan cults. Still others, while remaining in the church have begun attempts thoroughly to reform the church's life and thought. As one such reformer has stated:

> Christian theology and the Christian community will only be able to speak in an authentic way to the quest for feminist spirituality and for the religious identity of women when the whole church, as well as its individual members, has renounced all forms of sexist ideology and praxis which are exhibited in our church structures, theologies and liturgies. The Church has publicly to confess that it has wronged women.[3]

No appeal to biblical literalism or papal or hierarchical authority or traditional practice is sufficient to still such demand. Women are asking for the church's sincere affirmation in practice of the new life of freedom that they have received from their Lord. Surely that affirmation is part of the church's "reasonable service."

In reforming its thought and practice in order to affirm the equality of women, however, the church must proceed very knowledgeably, with an eye to the consequences of its actions, lest it destroy its gospel in the process of reform. Nowhere is this more true than in relation to the church's use of language about God. Surely the church can reform much of its language *about human beings* to include females in all its statements, despite the awkwardness of translating English generics into inclusive terms. As Letty Russell has pointed out, "It is generic nonsense to say that women are included linguistically when they are excluded by so many practices."[4] But the transformation of language *about God* is another problem altogether, as can be illustrated most tellingly from feminist theologies themselves.

To my knowledge, every feminist theology published in this country in the last two decades has called for the use of female terms for God. The argument has been that the Bible's use of masculine verbal images for the deity has been taken literally to legitimate the domination of women by men. "Since God is male, the male is God."[5] Further, when it has been rightly pointed out that God has no sexuality in the Bible, the answer has been in this vein:

> . . .I am quite aware that God is not really either female or male or anything in between. I only wish the people who argue to retain solely male imagery were as aware that God is not really male as I am that God is not really female. I am talking about the only thing we can talk about—images of God, not God.[6]

And of course the fact that Jesus Christ, the incarnate Son, was also male has only added to the problem especially when the Roman Catholic Church has decreed that women cannot therefore be ordained and represent Christ before the community.[7]

The feminist solution has been rather varied. Some writers simply use "she" and "her" in speaking of God and Christ.[8] For the Trinity of Father, Son, and Holy Spirit, some substitute Creator, Liberator, and Comforter,[9] and avoid the excessive use of terms such as Father, King, and Master by often substituting Yahweh or God or *Abba*.[10] In the much-discussed *An Inclusive Language Lectionary*,[11] the Bible's use of Father is changed to Father (and Mother), Lord to Sovereign, King to Ruler or Monarch, Son of Man to Human One, Son of God to Child of God. Rosemary Radford Ruether consistently calls the deity God/ess,[12] while Rita Gross uses God-She.[13] Others apply feminine usage only to the Holy Spirit or avoid the problem altogether by using impersonal terms for God, such as Wisdom, Glory, Holy One, Rock, Fire, First and Last, or neuter terms like Liberator, Maker, Defender, Friend, Nurturer. And Jesus is described as a male only in his earthly life, while he becomes Liberator, Redeemer, Savior in his representation of the new humanity.[14]

Those who employ such changes in the biblical usage justify them by pointing to female imagery for God in the Bible itself[15] or by claiming that the Catholic cult of Mary furnishes a tradition of female language and imagery in speaking of the divine.[16] "If we do not mean that God is male when we use masculine pronouns and imagery," asks Rita Gross, "then why should there be any objections to using female imagery and pronouns as well?"[17] ". . .female God language compels us to overcome the idolatrous equation of God with androcentric notions of humanity in a way that no other linguistic device can."[18]

The changes are not only linguistic devices, however. They also represent substantive alterations of the understanding of God. Gross herself talks about a "bisexual androgynous deity"[19] and Naomi Janowitz and Maggie Wening produced this Sabbath prayer for Jewish women:

Blessed is She who spoke and the world became. Blessed is She.
Blessed is She who in the beginning, gave birth. . . . . .
Blessed is She whose womb covers the earth.
Blessed is She whose womb protects all creatures. . . .[20]

The "Mother of the Womb" in this prayer gives birth to the universe. Virginia Mollenkott makes the same point in a discussion of the image of God as a mother eagle, which she finds in Gen. 1:2:

. . .the similar use of *rachapth* in Genesis and Deuteronomy makes it. . .probable that the very first image in the Bible is of God as a mother eagle fluttering over the waters as she gives birth to the universe.

In Egyptian hieroglyphics, the letter A is represented by the eagle, standing for the Origin of all things and the warmth of life. We are only reclaiming our biblical and cultural heritage when we see that origin not in terms of masculine impregnation, but rather in terms of feminine involvement in the birth and nurturing process. God is our mother-eagle. In her we safely put our trust.[21]

There is, of course, no thought in the Bible that a male God impregnates anything or anyone in order to bring forth creation, but it is typical of feminist theology that it speaks of a female deity giving birth to the world. *Indeed, when female terminology is used for God, the birthing image becomes inevitable*. Mollenkott can therefore push the image farther to talk of the God of Naomi, in the Book of Ruth, as "the God with Breasts," "the undivided One God who births and breast-feeds the universe."[22]

If a female deity gives birth to the universe, however, it follows that all things participate in the life or in the substance and divinity of that deity—in short, that *the creator is indissolubly bound up with the creation*. And this is exactly what one finds in feminist theologies. Thus, Rosemary Ruether speaks of ". . .the root human image of the divine as the Primal Matrix, the great womb within which all things, Gods and humans, sky and earth, human and nonhuman beings, are generated," —an image, she rightly says, which survives in the metaphor of the divine as Ground of Being.[23] But this is no mere image or metaphor for Ruether. This God/ess, as Ruether terms her, is divine reality: ". . .the empowering Matrix: She, in whom we live and move and have our being—She comes: She is here."[24]

The result of such imagery, then, is that human beings are considered to incarnate the divine:

Both sweet and bitter, Naomi and Mara, this woman [Naomi] incarnated the God. . .
Noami with all her limitations remained for Ruth the image-bearer of the undivided One God who births and breast-feeds the universe.[25]

"This is what the Goddess symbolizes—the divine within women and all that is female in the universe," writes Zsuzsanna E. Budapest.[26] Thus, in a "self-blessing ritual" she can say, "Bless my genitals that bring forth life as you have brought forth the universe," and then explain the statement in this way: ". . .we do give birth, we do issue forth people, just as the Goddess issues forth the universe. That is a biological connection and manifestation of the Goddess. . . And the responsibility you accept is that you are divine, and that you have power."[27] In similar fashion, Carol P. Christ maintains that the woman who says, "I found God in myself and I loved her fiercely," is saying ". . .that the divine principle, the saving and sustaining power, is in herself, that she will no longer look to men or male figures as saviors."[28]

The feminists disagree among themselves as to whether or not males too incarnate the divine—(many follow their own logic and maintain that they do)—but it also inevitably follows that if the deity is inseparably connected with the universe, then everything participates in the divine. And once again, such thought is part and parcel of feminist theology. "Our milieu" is "divine," maintains Mollenkott,[29] who claims to speak from biblical evidence. Actually, however, the presuppositions of her thought are little different from those of Starhawk, who writes out of the pagan context of modern witchcraft's covens:

> There is no dichotomy between spirit and flesh, no split
> between Godhead and the world. The Goddess is manifest
> in the world; she brings life into being, is Nature, is flesh.
> Union is not sought outside the world in some heavenly
> sphere or through dissolution of the self into the void
> beyond the senses. Spiritual union is found in life, within
> nature, passion, sensuality—
> through being fully human, fully one's self.
>
> Our great symbol for the Goddess is the moon, whose
> three aspects reflect the three stages in women's lives and
> whose cycles of waxing and waning coincide with women's
> menstrual cycles. . .
>
> The Goddess is also earth—Mother Earth, who sustains
> all growing things, who is the body, our bones and cells.
> She is air. . . fire. . . water. . .mare, cow, cat, owl, crane,
> flower, tree, apple, seed, lion, sow, stone, woman. She is
> found in the world around us, in the cycles and seasons of
> nature, and in mind, body, spirit, and the emotions within
> each of us. Thou art Goddess. I am Goddess. All that lives

(and all that is, lives), all that serves life, is Goddess.[30]

Such statements serve as a vivid summary of the end result of a religion in which creator and creation are undivided. And if female imagery for the deity is used, such beliefs are its logical outcome. They are also identical, however, with that mythopoeic thought known to every people before the advent of the Judaic-Christian faith. Let me explain.

Elaine Pagels is quite correct when she states that ". . .the absence of feminine symbolism of God marks Judaism, Christianity, and Islam in striking contrast to the world's other religious traditions, whether in Egypt, Babylonia, Greece and Rome, or Africa, Polynesia, India, and North America."[31] And the reason for that is that in most of the cultures of the world, deity and world are not differentiated. Rather, the divine is bound up with and revealed through the natural world; indeed, in ancient Mesopotamia the gods and goddesses were thought to emanate out of chaotic matter. Thus, not only the Babylonians, but also the Egyptians and Greeks and Romans saw in the manifestations of nature the life and activity of the deities. The expanse of the sky, the heat of the sun, the growth and death of vegetation, the fury of the storm—these were to these ancient peoples not impersonal happenings and objects, but cosmic Thou's which affected human life and demanded adjustment to them. Nature was alive for primitive peoples (and still is, for many modern people). Its changes were due to divine will. Its conflicts were the struggles of opposing gods and goddesses. Its harmony was the result of the organization of the cosmic, divine state, as in Mesopotamian theology. Or its harmony stemmed from the genealogical relationships of the deities, as in Hesiod's *Theogony*.

To explain this vital and personal world around them, ancient peoples therefore constructed myths—the stories of gods and goddesses—such as the story of Marduk and Tiamat. That explained the origin of the universe, and to preserve the universe, the ancient Babylonians would then act out the story of the defeat of Tiamat in the cult, thus ensuring by the practice of sympathetic magic that the world would be preserved. The theory was that "like produced like"—what was done in the cult coerced the world of nature and deities to do likewise. The exercise of human fertility in the cult of sacred prostitution, for example, was thought to coerce fertility in the natural world (a thought not at all at odds with Starhawk's statement about goddess religion: "In orgasm, we share in the force that moves the stars"[32]). Or the ritual dramatization of the resurrection of Baal was thought to restore nature's bounty. The natural world reflected the life of the divine, and by harmonizing with that world and influencing it through cultic ritual, human beings entered into the "Primal Matrix" of all life and used it to their advantage.

The realm of the deities in such myths was timeless—what has been called "durative" by Theodor Gaster, over against the "punctual" time of earth. However, this timeless realm of the gods and goddesses was then thought to be reflected in nature's cycle, which was also seen to be an unending circle of birth, life, and death. In other words, in mythopoeic thought, nature's cycle was the pattern for human history, and human life also endlessly repeated itself in the never-ending natural cycles of birth, life, and death. Outside of biblical thought, such a cyclical understanding of history remained the classical tradition until the time of Darwin, when it was seen that nature not only repeated itself but also evolved in newness. In many philosophies, the cycle of nature therefore came to be viewed as a spiral, to allow for the introduction of novelty. Nevertheless, nature remained the pattern for human life. And significantly, it is to this cyclical view of history that feminist Sheila Collins wants to return:" . . .the exclusivity of the linear view of history dissolves, and other paradigms begin to assume an ontological and existential importance for us; for example, the cyclical view of history becomes once again a possibility."[33]

It should give feminist theologians pause, however, to realize that many cultures have found a cyclical or spiral view of human history to be meaningless, and that therefore the attempt of religion and philosophy in many of those cultures has been to escape out of such history. In India and China, the goal of life has been to escape out of the meaninglessness of a circular history into the timeless realm of Nirvana, a solution which implies that everyday life has no meaning. In the philosophies of Plato and Aristotle, the escape from history is rational, and human beings take refuge from the circle of life by retreating into the realm of pure form. In modern philosophies, such as those of Nietzsche and Spengler, the only alternative is nobly to assert, if finally futilely, individual freedom. In Nietzsche, this leads to suicide, in Spengler to a form of fatalism. But whatever the particular point of view, not one of these positions is positive, no one of them holding that the common life we live on this earth in time has any meaning. Life is, for a person with a circular history, finally "a tale told by an idiot, full of sound and fury, signifying nothing." This is very close to what we find also in some forms of modern existentialism, and it is the view of that branch of modern drama known as the Absurd Theater. In Beckett's *Waiting for Godot*, for example, no action takes place because all action is meaningless. Life goes around in a circle and finally means nothing. History is an endless repetition of events, having no goal or purpose—a meaninglessness which is vividly portrayed in Ecclesiastes. 1:2-11.

For the first time in history, however, in a way that remains unique in the world, the Judaic, Christian, biblical faith (imitated by Islam) overcomes the tyranny of nature's spiral, and the whole mythopoeic understanding of God and the world is dissolved. This can be seen most clearly from Genesis 1. There the priestly writers borrow fragments of the myth of the chaos dragon (Tiamat), but they completely demythologize the borrowed material. First, God is the only God, and so there is no struggle involved between deities. God's creation is effortless. He speaks, and the world comes to be.

Second, God does not emanate out of the chaotic matter, nor is he contained in or bound up with his creation in any way. Rather, he stands over and above his world as its sovereign Lord and Creator. This is emphasized in the biblical account in three ways: 1) by the repeated use of the Hebrew term *bara'*, which is used in the Bible only of God's creative activity—an activity which cannot be comprehended within or derived from the structures of creation; 2) by the fact that the only instrument of God's creation is his spoken word (cf. John 1. Between God and the world stands the Word. The world does not emanate out of him or contain some part of his being within it. He has not implanted divinity within any parts of the creation, not even in human beings, and therefore no created thing and no created person can be claimed to be divine); 3) the world is the object addressed by God the subject (cf. Isa. 1:2; 40:22, 26; Mic. 6:2 et al.).

Third, Genesis 1 abandons mythopoeic thought by placing the creation within time. Not only are the individual acts of creation divided among seven days, but the creation of the world is made the beginning of the sacred history, and this is marked in the priestly account by the scheme of *toledoth* or generations (Gen. 2:4a; 5:1; 6:9; 10:1). The time of nature is therefore subjected to the time of God's purpose. In other biblical texts, therefore, far from being the measure and pattern of human history, nature itself is subjected to that history and is dependent on God's salvation within history (cf.e.g. Isa. 11:6-9; 55:12; Jer. 12:4; Ps. 98:7-9; Rom. 8:19-21).

These biblical understandings of God's relation to his creation are enormously important, then, for Christian faith and life. First, because God is not bound up with his creation in any way, creation may pass away but God does not pass away (cf. Pss. 102:25-27; 46:1-2; Isa. 51:6; 54:10; Mark 13:31 pars.). He therefore is able to take those who love him into a fellowship with himself that abides eternally (John 11:25; 14:1-3). In an atomic age, when the push of a button may return the world to *tohu wabbohu*—unordered chaos (cf. Jer. 4:23-26)—that faith alone makes it possible to say, "Therefore we will not fear" (Ps.46:2).

Second, because God is not bound up with or revealed through the created world, but is revealed only through his own Word (whose meaning includes his acts), nature's processes and structures are not revelatory of the nature of God. If they were, then we could pretty well conclude that the big gods eat the little gods, that death is as much a part of the divine purpose as is life, and that, judging from the deity's supposed "incarnation" in human beings, God is evil as well as good. The Bible knows better, and so it refuses to identify God with his world. According to the second commandment of the Decalogue, we cannot find him revealed through "anything that is in heaven above, or that is in the earth beneath, or that is in the water under the earth" (Exod. 20:4), and both the Deuteronomic history and the prophetic writings consistently judge in the harshest terms those fertility and goddess religions that would deny God's otherness from his creation (cf. Rom. 1:22-24). The God of the Bible is "holy" God, qualitatively different from all creation.

(It might be noted, incidentally, that this differentiation of God from his world and the demytholigization of the creation comprise a world view that alone has made it possible for Western science and technology to work with the material world. If the world is divine, you dare not tamper with it, and so rats eat up a third of India's food supply each year—the Christian faith makes a difference in how human beings live! Further, however, there is no thought in the Scriptures that human beings can mistreat the earth. The world belongs to God: "The earth is the Lord's and the fullness thereof" (Ps. 24:1), and human beings are always responsible to God for their stewardship of the creation. We are, as Psalm 39 so marvelously puts it, God's "passing guests" upon the earth).

Third, because nature's time is subject to God's time, the purpose of human life is given to it, therefore, not by nature's cycle of unending repetition but by the historical movement forward of

God's purpose to create his kingdom of love and goodness on earth. And human beings may choose to cooperate with and further that purpose or they may oppose it and fight against it. In other words, everyday human decisions and actions have cosmic and eternal significance. By what we do and say, we can influence the course (though not the final outcome) of God's purpose and our relation to it, not only for ourselves but for others and for all creation. By how we decide and act, we can affirm the eternal life or death of ourselves, of others, and of the universe. What we do—everyday!—makes a difference—eternally!—for all persons and things.

Nor are our decisions and labors as specific individuals insignificant in the cosmic scheme of God's purpose. Rosemary Ruether has this to say in her God/ess religion about personal eschatology:

> In effect (at death), our existence ceases as individuated ego/organism and dissolves back into the cosmic matrix of matter/energy, from which new centers of individuation arise. It is this matrix, rather than our individuated centers of being, that is "everlasting," that subsists underneath the coming to be and passing away of individuated beings and even planetary worlds. Acceptance of death, then, is acceptance of the finitude of our individuated centers of being, but also our identification with the larger matrix as our total self that contains us all. . . .To the extent to which we have transcended egoism for relation to community, we can also accept death as the final relinquishment of individuated ego into the great matrix of being.[34]

Theoretically, that may appeal to some, but it gives no help at the side of a grave, when a grieving husband and children ask, "Will we ever see her again?"—that is, it gives no help whatsoever in the very context of love and community. Nor does it give any meaning to the question of, Why you? Why do you—you yourself, with your individual fingerprints and voice and expressions, you with your particular talents and thoughts and personality, you with your consciuosness and no one else's—why do you exist? Is there a particular purpose for your creation? And is that then a transitory purpose, expressed solely in a brief "individuation," which disappears into the undifferentiated cosmic matrix of matter/energy?

> Remember that thou hast made me of clay;
> and wilt thou turn me to dust again? (Job.10:9).

Does the person that is you become undifferentiated, unknown, and finally—because eternally—unimportant? That would seem to make the struggle fully to become oneself hardly worthwhile. Why the thousand peculiar sufferings and labors, thoughts and dreams, struggles and anxieties of each individual human life? For that matter, why the cares and work of any ordinary mother—the hours spent, the noses blown, the skinned knees bandaged, the talents encouraged, the assurance and comfortings given to bring up a child if the "individuation" does not matter in some eternal purpose for the world?

But the testimony of biblical faith is that the individual does matter—that the Good Shepherd knows his own and his own know him, and that each individual life is held precious—the very hairs on our heads each numbered—within the context of a beloved community that has one flock and one Shepherd (John 10:14-18)—a beloved community that will abide, moreover, to all eternity (John 17:24). When looked at realistically, God/ess religion and all those like it, cheapen the value of human life, because finally death renders the particular expressions of that life meaningless.

There are other contrasts that could be drawn between feminist theology and the biblical faith, and they too stem finally from feminist refusal to differentiate Creator from creation. For example, because feminist theology understands human beings to participate in or incarnate the divine within themselves, there is little realistic understanding of the nature of human sin. Dorothee Soelle rejects any idea of a "fall";

> Coming out is liberation. Let us read the story of Adam and Eve as a coming out. The first human beings come out and discover themselves; they discover the joy of learning, the pleasures of beauty and knowledge. Let us praise Eve, who brought this about. Without Eve we would still be sitting in the trees. Without her curiosity we would not know what knowledge was.[35]

God then, for Soelle, is love within human beings: "God is our capacity to love. God is the power, the spark, that animates our love. . . We should stop looking for God. He has been with us for a long time."[36] Therefore, according to Soelle, we are strong, we can accomplish things, we are not dispensable, we can create a new social order and a new world: "We do not have to sit around all year singing, with Luther, 'Did we in our own strength confide, our striving would be losing.'"[37] "To live, we do not need what has repeatedly been called 'God,' a power that intervenes, rescues,

judges, and confirms. The most telling argument against our traditional God is not that he no longer exists or that he has drawn back
within himself but that we no longer need him. We do not need him
because love is all we need, nothing more."[38] Such a thought is,
says Soelle,

> . . .the central idea in the Bible.
> The tradition has added Christology and ecclesiology to
> it, the virgin birth, the resurrection and the ascension, the
> Trinity, original sin, and eternity. . . .
> I do not think we can restore this language, this house of
> language. I think we will have to let this house fall apart,
> that we will have to abandon it in the condition it is in and
> build a new one on this one simple foundation: All you need
> is love.[39]

To the contrary, however, in a world where human torture is
the rule in most prisons, where a person on a subway platform in
New York City can push a woman in front of an oncoming train
"just for the hell of it," where little children in a nursery school can
be tied up and sexually abused, where whole races can be uprooted
or starved to death or burnt up in gas ovens, it must be said that
Soellee's is a naive understanding indeed, and that we do indeed
need a Power greater than human evil, or for that matter a Power
greater than even the highest human love and good, for it was the
best religion and the best law that erected the cross on Golgotha. If
there is not a God, who is Lord over life, who "intervenes, rescues,
judges, and confirms," and who has given his final judgment and
won his decisive victory in the cross and resurrection of Jesus
Christ, then human evil will always have the last word and there is
no hope for this world. Liberal feminists, like some liberals in other
movements, maintain that they can, by their own power, restruc-
ture society, restore creation, and overcome suffering. But as Reinhold Niebuhr used to say to us, in so many words, about Marxism's
equally naive dreams, "They have no understanding of that human
sin which will defeat the revolution."

The point is, however, that all these feminist errors—indeed,
all this feminist rejection of God and its resulting idolatry—are built
on the theological misstep of identifying God with his creation.
And that misstep becomes inevitable when the feminists reject any
notion of the inspiration of the canonical witness to God,[40] make
their own experience their authority,[41] and use female language
for God. As soon as God is called female, the images of birth, of
suckling, of carrying in the womb, and, most importantly, the

identification of the deity with the life in all things become inevitable, and the Bible's careful and consistent distinction between Creator and creation is blurred and lost.

It must puzzle those feminist theologians, who appeal to the prophets' championship of the oppressed,[42] that the prophets nevertheless never address God as female, quite sparingly use female metaphors to picture God's activity, and indeed, condemn the worship of all goddesses. It is not that the prophets were slaves to their patriarchal culture, as some feminists hold. And it is not that the prophets *could not* imagine God as female; they were surrounded by peoples who so imaged their deities! It is rather than the prophets, as well as the Deuteronomists and Priestly writers and Jesus and Paul, *would not* use such language, because they knew and had ample evidence from the religions surrounding them that female language for the deity results in a basic distortion of the nature of God and of his relation to his creation. And surely, contemporary feminist theologies themselves are a demonstration of the truth of that statement! Paul, in writing of the human race, put his finger precisely on the source of all idolatry: ". . .they. . .worshiped and served the creature rather than the Creator. . ." (Rom. 1:25).

As the church struggles with the issue of women's full equality, therefore—and struggle it must to insure that equality, if it wishes to live up to its gospel—let it therefore divide the wheat from the tares in the demands women are making of it. Those who have been denied their proper freedom and justice can sometimes be as sinfully wrong in their demands as are their oppressors, and the church must be guided in its liberation of women by the canon of the Bible that remains its sure authority for all faith and practice. Moreover, that guide must be used, not according to the letter, but according to the Spirit,[43] lest it too be employed as an instrument of oppression, as has so often been the case. The church cannot and it must not accede to feminist demands that language about God be changed to feminine, for then the church will have lost that God in whom it truly lives and moves and has its being.

In addition, if the church accedes to feminist demands for feminine language about God, it will also lose its proper servant role in the world. This becomes clear when one examines in feminist theologies these women's understanding of their own role. By eliminating the difference between Creator and creation, and by understanding themselves as incarnations of the divine, many feminists have declared their freedom from any sort of rule, *including God's.*

In an imaginative picture of Mary Magdalene in the preface to her book, Rosemary Ruether sets forth such ideas:

> Perhaps it is this very idea of God as a great king, ruling over nations as His servants, that has been done away with by Jesus' death on the cross. With Jesus' death, God, the heavenly Ruler, has left the heavens and has been poured out upon the earth with his blood. A new God is being born in our hearts to teach us to level the heavens and exalt the earth and create a new world without masters and slaves, rulers and subjects. . . .

> "But who will be ready to hear this message?" Mary thought. "Although Jesus had emptied the throne of God, even now Peter and some of the other disciples are busy trying to fill it again. They will fashion the Risen Jesus into a new Lord and Master to represent the heavenly Father and to rule upon the earth. Oh yes, they will be his humble servants." Mary shuddered. "Is there any way to rend this fabric, to let the light of this other world shine through? Perhaps something of this other vision will still get through the distortion."[44]

The central affirmation of the Christian Church, the lordship of Jesus Christ, at whose name finally every knee will bow and every tongue confess (Phil. 2:10-11), is understood as a distortion of the biblical witness!

In the same vein, liberationist and mystic Dorothee Soelle rejects all service of such a Lord:

> In the mystical tradition, there is no room for deferring to a higher power, for worshiping alien rule, and for denying our own strength. On the contrary, mystical texts often explicity criticize the master-servant relationship; and their primary way of doing this is through a creative use of language.

> Here, religion is a sense of unity with the whole, a sense of belonging, not of submitting. We do not honor God because of his power over us; we immerse ourselves in him, in his love, as mystical language often puts it. He is, as Meister Eckhart says, the fundament, love, the depths, the sea. Symbols from nature are preferred where our relationship with God is not one of obedience but of unity, where we are not subject to the commands of some remote being that demands sacrifice and the relinquishing of the self, but rather where we are asked to become one with all of life.[45]

Few quotations more concisely summarize the views of feminist theology: the loss of distinction between Creator and creation, the resulting emphasis on oneness with all life in nature and in the deity, the absolutizing of the individual's capacities, the denial of sin, and finally, therefore, the absolutizing of the individual's own self-rule.

In all fairness, let it be said that most of these feminist theologians with whom we have dealt have a lively social ethic dedicated to the elimination of oppression and injustice from the earth, concern for the environment, a reliance on the support and direction of feminine communities, and a remarkable tolerance toward differing feminist viewpoints. Most of them also acknowledge that none of their formulations are final and that feminist theology is highly experimental and experiential. They are pragamatic in the extreme. Some of them will borrow any view that seems to liberate women, whether such view be found in the paganism of modern witchcraft or the early Christian heresies of Montanism and Gnosticism. But finally, each of them is operating out of the authority of her own individual experience, informed by some "sisterhood," beholden to no God other than herself and the goddess created in her own imagination. This absolutizing of women's own subjectivity is vividly illustrated by a passage by Carol Christ:

> Some would assert that the Goddess definitely is not "out there," that the symbol of a divinity "out there" is part of the legacy of patriarchal oppression, which brings with it authoritarianism, hierarchicalism, and dogmatic rigidity associated with biblical monotheist religions. They might assert that the Goddess symbol reflects the sacred power within women and nature, suggesting the connectedness between women's cycles of menstruation, birth, and menopause, and the life and death cycles of the universe. Others seem quite comfortable with the notion of Goddess as a divine female protector and creator and would find their experience of Goddess limited by the assertion that she is not also out there as well as within themselves and in all natural processes. When asked what the symbol of Goddess means, feminist priestess Starhawk replied, "It all depends on how I feel. When I feel weak, she is someone who can help and protect me. When I feel strong, she is the symbol of my own power. At other times I feel her as the natural energy in my body and the world" . . . . Theologians might call these the words of a sloppy thinker. But my deepest in-

tuition tells me they contain a wisdom (sic) that Western theological thought has lost.[46]

Valerie Saiving has maintained that theologians such as Reinhold Niebuhr and Anders Nygren, who have defined sin as pride and the will-to-power and grace as sacrificial love, have been influenced by their own masculinity, have failed to illumine women's experience, and have reinforced "women's sin" of self-forgetfulness and self-negation.[47] But there is little self-negation on the part of a woman who claims to incarnate the divine and who has made her own experience her authority for dividing truth from untruth. On the contrary, such a woman has, as Genesis 3 so long ago portrayed it, desired "to be like God." Perhaps we could say that modern feminism has now reversed the ancient story. In the original story, Adam followed Eve's lead, in the sin of complicity. But now males "lord" it over females and females want to follow that lead, making of themselves their own gods and their own arbitors of right and wrong.

Human beings are not gods, however. They are creatures, created by a wise and loving and good Creator, who desires so much, despite their sin, that they have abundant life, that he has been willing to sacrifice his only begotten Son to give them that life. Within that role of creature, guided by the wisdom and forgiven, redeemed, and sustained by the power of a God who is perfect love, there is indeed an abundant life to be had of joy and meaning, of mutual service among human beings, of fulfillment and use of one's highest capacities, and of perfect freedom. When one reads feminist theologies, one has the feeling that their authors, with a few exceptions, have never really known what it is to live that abundant life of freedom given us by Jesus Christ. Part of that is due to the strenuous and persistent hold that sin has upon us, but part of it is also due to the fact that the church, in relation to females, has not always proclaimed and acted out its good news of justice and righteousness and peace and freedom for all persons.

All of us, female and male, are called by Jesus Christ to equal discipleship in the service of his gospel. We are indeed his servants in the world, and he is our Lord. And part of the service of that Lord is the willingness to follow him and to be crucified by the sin in the world—*females not exempted*. Christians, like their Lord, have always been crucified; they always will be. But let the church not add to that sin by crucifying its own female disciples! Let it acknowledge, rather, in word and deed, that Jesus Christ has set all us captives free. And yet, at the same time, let the church also be careful, in proclaiming its good news that it does not change the Word of God into mere human words and thereby destroy its own gospel.

Notes

1. Cf. for example, Raymond E. Brown, S.S., "Roles of Women in the Fourth Gospel," *Woman: New Dimensions,* edited by Walter Burkhardt, S.J. (New York: Paulist Press, 1975), pp.112-123; Elisabeth Schuessler Fiorenza, *In Memory of Her: A Feminist Theological Reconstruction of Christian Origins* (New York: Crossroad, 1983).

2. Raden Adjeng Kartini, a pioneer in the struggle for Indonesian independence and liberation of women through educational reform, 1899. Quoted by Letty M. Russell, *Human Liberation in A Feminist Perspective—A Theology (Philadelphia: Westminster Press, 1974), p.18.*

3. Elisabeth Schuessler Fiorenza, "Feminist Spirituality, Christian Identity, and Catholic Vision," *Womanspirit Rising: A Feminist Reader in Religion,* edited by Carol P. Christ and Judith Plaskow (San Francisco: Harper and Row, 1979), p.147. (Subsequent footnotes will refer to this word as *Womanspirit Rising*).

4. *Op. cit.,* p. 95.

5. Mary Daly, "The Qualitative Leap Beyond Patriarchal Religion," in *Quest* (Women and Spirituality), 1974, Volume I, p.21.

6. Rita Gross, "Female God Language in a Jewish Context," *Womanspirit Rising,* p.168.

7. Cf. Fiorenza, *Womanspirit Rising,* p. 137.

8. Cf. Fiorenza, *In Memory of Her,* pp. 345, 347.

9. Cf. Russell, *op. cit.,* p. 102.

10. Russell. "Changing Language and the Church," *The Liberating Word: A Guide to Nonsexist Interpretation of the Bible,* edited by Letty M. Russell (Philadelphia: The Westminster Press, 1976), p. 92.

11. Published for the Cooperative Publication Association by John Knox Press, Atlanta; The Pilgrim Press, New York; The Westminster Press, Philadelphia, 1983-85.

12. *Sexism and God-Talk: Toward a Feminist Theology* (Boston: Beacon Press, 1983).

13. Cf. *Womanspirit Rising,* p. 173.

14. Cf. Russell, "Changing Language and the Church," *op. cit.,* p. 93.

15. Cf. for example, Phyllis Trible, *God and the Rhetoric of Sexuality* (Philadelphia: Fortress Press, 1978); Virginia Ramey Mollenkott, *The Divine Feminine: The Biblical Imagery of God as Female* (New York: Crossroad, 1983). Parts of Mollenkott's discussion are unfortunately marred by serious inadequacies in biblical exegesis. Cf. the discussion of Jesus' cry from the cross, p. 33, or the treatment of "the Bakerwoman God" in relation to John 6:31-35, p. 81.

16. Cf. Fiorenza, *Womanspirit Rising,* p. 139.

17. *Womanspirit Rising,* p. 170.

18. *Ibid.,* pp. 171-172.

19. *Ibid.,* p. 168.

20. "Sabbath Prayers for Women," *Womanspirit Rising*, p. 176.

21. *Op. cit.*, pp. 89-90.

22. *Ibid.*, p. 58.

23. *Op. cit.*, pp. 48-49.

24. *Ibid.*, p. 266.

25. Mollenkott, *op. cit.*, pp. 57-58.

26. "Self-Blessing Ritual," *Womanspirit Rising*, p. 272.

27. *Ibid.*, p. 271.

28. "Why Women Need the Goddess: Phenomenological, Psychological, and Political Reflections," *Womanspirit Rising*, p. 277.

29. *Op cit.*, p. 109.

30. "Witchcraft and Women's Culture," *Womanspirit Rising*, p. 263.

31. "What Became of God the Mother? Conflicting Images of God in Early Christianity," *Womanspirit Rising*, p. 107.

32. *The Spiral Dance: A Rebirth of the Ancient Religion of the Great Goddess* (San Francisco: Harper and Row, 1979), p. 196.

33. "Reflections on the Meaning of Herstory," *Womanspirit Rising*, p. 70.

34. *Op cit.*, pp. 257-258.

35. *The Strength of the Weak: Toward a Christian Feminist Identity*, translated by Robert and Rita Kimber (Philadelphia: Westminster Press, 1984), p. 126.

36. *Ibid.*, p. 138.

37. *Ibid.*, p. 158.

38. *Ibid.*, p.137.

39. *Ibid.*, pp. 133-134.

40. Cf. for example, Ruether, *op. cit.*, p. 17; Christ, *op. cit.*, p. 230.

41. Cf. for example, Collins, *op. cit.*, p. 69; Soelle, *op. cit.*, p. 87; Ruether, *op. cit.*, pp. 18-19; Noami R. Goldenberg. "Dreams and Fantasies as Sources of Revelation: Feminist Appropriation of Jung." *Womanspirit Rising*, pp. 219-226.

42. Cf. for example, Ruether, *op. cit.*, p. 23.

43. A discussion of the proper interpretation of the Scriptures would lead us far afield from the subject of this article, and there is no space to give to it. Let it simply be said that although the Bible's message comes to us out of the context of a patriarchal world, its good news is a consistent and emphatic confirmation of the equality of women before God and therefore in human society.

44. *Op. cit.*, pp. 10-11.

45. *Op. cit.*, p. 102.

46. "Why Women Need the Goddess," *Womanspirit Rising* pp. 278-279.

47. "The Human Situation: A Feminine View," *Womanspirit Rising, passim*. Summarized also on pp. 20-21.

Next to the Last Link:
The Preacher in the Process of Interpretation
by F. Wellford Hobbie

"Next to the last link" is the intriguing phrase Richard Rohrbaugh uses to describe the preacher's involvement in the "hermeneutical chain" stretching from the biblical passage through the varied scholarly processes to the person doing the interpretation for the church.[1] The pastor sitting in the study before a biblical passage, looking forward to the proclamation of the Word to the congregation next Sunday, is the "next to the last link." The "last link," of course, is when the listener in the congregation hears and understands that the word spoken has his or her name upon it, and words became the Word. Then the hermeneutical chain is complete, and, as Dietrich Bonhoeffer has said, "Christ walks through the congregation as the Word."[2] But our focus will be upon that "next to the last link" in interpretation, upon the preacher sitting, seemingly in lonely isolation, before a biblical passage with the inevitability of next Sunday's worship and proclamation looming on the horizon.

It is appropriate indeed for a focus such as this to be in a *Festchrift* for Professor Mays, for much of his work in hermeneutics has been motivated to serve the preacher, teacher, and interpreter in the fellowship of the community of faith. This has been his focus. But there is a hesitancy in writing about this moment of interpretation which comes from the realization that clearly one of the most competent persons to address this area is Professor Mays himself. Some wag once said that "there should not be a chair of homiletics in a seminary, but a bench." Professor Mays has occupied an honored place on the "bench of homiletics" in his seminary teaching. His contributions to both students and teachers have been significant in the interpretive moves from a biblical passage to a sermon. One could only wish that he were the one addressing the subject now. Perhaps a contribution of this paper may be to motivate him to correct the flaws in this attempt by describing more adequately the crucial link in the hermeneutical chain.

I

Crucial though this moment of interpretation may be, relatively few have given it focused attention. Of course every "how to" book on homiletics recognizes the importance of the preacher in the moves "from text to sermon," and certainly material abounds describing the exegetical process of critically studying the passage. What is lacking is an emphasis upon and an analysis of those ambiguities of the relationships between exegesis of the passage, systematic theology, and the contemporary culture and its ideologies. What is lacking is an investigation of precisely what influences the preacher before a passage.

That this is a neglected area is understandable. After all, such an attempt ultimately probes into the perilous maze of "subjectivism." Here one is challenged to venture beyond the objective procedures of exegesis into the preacher's creedal stance, presuppositions, and ideologies. Here one goes beyond the critical analysis of the passage to seek these inner influences affecting the preacher. Anyone attempting to sort this out may find himself or herself ultimately in the quandary of the centipede:

A centipede was happy quite
Until a frog in fun
Said, "Pray which leg comes after which?"
This raised her mind to such a pitch
She lay distracted in a ditch,
Considering how to run.

Usually the minister goes along in this interpretive procedure quite oblivious of forces at work, but if someone asks "which comes after which?" the preacher may be as paralyzed as the centipede.

But, more seriously, hesitation may be due to the fact that this point of interpretation may defy description. Indeed, one would be well advised to cease and desist if the goal were to describe one methodology to be used by preachers. Karl Barth recognized the vanity of our endless discussion of a process of interpretation when he stated: "Hermeneutics cannot be an independent topic of conversation: its problem can only be tackled and answered in countless acts of interpretation—all of which are mutually corrective and supplementary, while all the time being principally concerned with the content of the text."[3]

II

But despite the admonishment of Barth and an agreement on the ambiguities and difficulties, the task of analysis and reflection on "the next to last link" deserves attention for two reasons.

First, because for many committed to preaching biblically, this is *the* wasteland. A preacher, adequately trained in exegetical procedures, in language, in the basic elements of the grammatico-historical process, often finds the results of his or her efforts disturbingly sterile. There on the desk are the facts gleaned from study. But something is lacking. Assiduous working with the passage too often ends in frustration. Professor Mays has described the experience of many a preacher:

> But because exegesis had set a pre-eminent value on the "historical" and did not see how to apply the term to the present form of texts, it has been too much content with the resulting fragmentation, has lingered among literary fragments and sources, archeological ruins, etymological roots, religious phenomenology—and not found the way back. Who among us has not sat helpless and amazedly distraught before the catalogue of results recorded in a critical commentary, unable to see the passage before us any longer, unable because the commentator insists on going behind it and knows no guide for the return, and return we must.[4]

Something is missing. A passage which at one time seemed vital and vibrant, pressing for proclamation, now may resemble a cadaver in an anatomy class: organs all identified and classified, neatly laid out, but with no resemblance to life nor possibility of resuscitation. So, far too many times, preaching from a biblical passage becomes a lecture, a recital of facts from the passage lacking the power and vitality of confrontation with the Word.

The second reason this analysis of the preacher's role is of central importance is that a disturbing number of preachers assume that they are "biblical preachers" when in reality their sermons are not reflections of the biblical passage. They may indeed have the biblical passage central in study and in the worship service, but "something has happened on the way to the pulpit." Ideas, concepts, ideologies quite foreign to the passage have intruded. The passage read prior to preaching has little or no relation to the affirmations of the sermon. The fault often is in the process of interpretation, in the give and take of minister with passage. We need to focus more upon what is taking place as the minister sits before the passage in the "next to the last link" to see if we can understand something of the forces at work.

III

If one attempts to analyze the hermeneutics involved when the minister sits down before the biblical passage and begins those last moves leading up to proclamation, one basic fact is evident. This interpretive work is carried on in what may be called "a community of faith" and is affected by a number of participants. The preacher may look quite alone there in the study. There before him or her on the desk is the scripture passage from which the Word will be proclaimed, but unseen, sitting around the desk, is a "community of participants" affecting in varying degrees the way the interpretive process will develop. There is at the center of it all the passage and its author, known or unknown, attempting to speak again the words, through the thousands of intervening years, to today. There is the preacher, not at all the *tabula rasa* freed from ideologies, theologies, and presuppositions which will have their say in the process. There is all about the preacher the congregation to whom the sermon will be preached, and there are the voices of the culture of the present age. All of these play a part in the act of interpretation. To omit any one of these in the dialogue of interpretation is impossible; to be unaware of the influences they bring is to run the risk of distorting or blunting interpretation.

All are at the study desk. They form, as it were, a "hermeneutical circle," a dialogue with the passage at the center and in the ascendancy. Each one participates in the interpretive conversation. But the matter is made more complex because participation is not orderly. One may *write* a sermon with the classical orderly form *explicatio-applicatio* and may use the overused transitional phrase: "But what does the passage have to say to us today?" But the truth of the matter is that at the first moment of interpretation when the preacher comes to the passage, he or she comes with a congregation. The preacher cannot leave the members of the congregation outside the study door in *interpretation*. They are the ones who must be involved at the outset, for they are those who will be before the pulpit next Sunday with their successes and failures, their joys and sorrows, their belief and disbelief. The first reading of the passage sees them there at the preacher's elbow.

Interpretation, then, for the preacher is a community participation and not easily described in an orderly fashion. The image of the circle of participants around the study desk, each one entering into dialogue in the search for meaning, is perhaps the most helpful. First the passage affirms its basic meaning from the initial reading, but this may collide with a long held presupposition of the preacher; then from a member of the congregation comes a question of clarity and the voicing of a pastoral concern, demanding again the listening afresh to the affirmation of the passage. On and on the interpretive conversation flows. The process is alive and flexible, making it quite impossible to describe a linear point-by-point procedure or anything resembling a model "from text to sermon."

Perhaps the best that can be done is to attempt to describe the participants in the process, the roles they play, their contributions and their potential threats in the final proclamation of the Word. The major participants we have identified are the preacher, the biblical passage, and the congregation.

We will now turn our attention to two of these—to the preacher and to the congregation. They are selected not because of their priority but because of the lack of attention and analysis they have received in the interpretive process. Clearly the central authoritative participant in the process should be the biblical passage, and for this reason it has deservedly received the most attention. Suffice it to say for our purposes that we shall assume that the passage's basic meaning is sought, using the best procedures of the grammatical-historical method. That is, the language of the passage in the light of the historical situation in which it was first written is sought to determine as nearly as possible the precise meaning of the passage and its central theological affirmations.[5] The biblical passage, let it be clearly understood, is assumed to stand always at the center; it is its Word the preacher seeks to hear; it is its authority that is ultimate. Our lack of attention in this paper to the grammatical-historical process applied to a biblical passage is not to be seen as demeaning its importance. Indeed, some of the brightest and best minds in the service of the church have given themselves to this process. The wealth of material available analyzing and describing each facet of it testifies to this. This paper simply assumes the central importance of the passage and the necessity of the preacher's commitment to careful exegesis. Our focus, however, will be upon a rather neglected area in the interpretive process—the factors impinging upon interpretation centered in preacher and congregation.[6]

IV

First, then, let us focus upon the preacher. There is a pressing need for the preacher to have a high level of self-understanding in the process of interpretation. There seemed to be an assumption in the early days of grammatico-historical emphases that the way to "correct exegesis" was freedom from any creedal or dogmatic presuppositions. Only by "cleansing oneself" from such presuppositions could one then be free to discover the meaning of the passage. But there was a failure to see that one cannot be rid of presuppositions. Indeed, "to sweep the house clean" of one set of presuppositions, such as "dogmatic assertions," simply invites others in. Each interpreter brings to a passage conscious or unconscious presuppositions. We, as well as the passage before us, have a history. Our ethical principles, theological beliefs, ideologies make their impact felt throughout the interpretive process.[7]

What is needed is not a denial of these presuppositions but a recognition and identification of their presence, a knowledge of our values, so that theological positions are brought into dialogue with the passage before us. As Professor Mays described it:

> He (the interpreter) has, in a word, presuppositions, but if there is inherent and justifiable validity to the situation of the exegete—if he is aware of his dominant presuppositions and holds them in the position of presuppositions so that they are always subject to the testing of confrontation with the material—then they do not cripple and confound the possibility of reaching the real meaning of a passage. Rather they are a part of the indispensable for doing so.[8]

Presuppositions are then to be recognized and enlisted in the search for meaning. The challenge is to identify them and to begin to understand how they function in the process.

If one understands a presupposition to be a "preliminary assumption, an antecedent logical condition,"[9] then it follows that in interpretation the interpreter does bring to a biblical passage "presuppositions" which affect profoundly the process and result of interpretation. There is, for example, a world of difference in the preacher's coming to a biblical passage to discover a word to be proclaimed in the midst of a community of faith gathered in worship and the biblical scholar sitting before the same passage looking upon it only as a literary piece to be analyzed historically, structurally, and linguistically. Both undertakings may be legitimate and both may follow certain similarities in exegetical procedures, but their differing presuppositions bring about different results. One, the biblical scholar, sees the passage as a source of objective research and may end up with an array of facts about the passage. The other, the preacher, sees the passage as a Word to be proclaimed, a witness of the living God to his people. The fundamental distinction that makes all the difference is the starting-point and the realization that here neutrality is not possible.[10]

The starting-point of interpretation differs not only between the biblical scholar coming to the passage as "an object" to be analyzed to satisfy historical and linguistic questions and the preacher coming to the same passage searching in it for a word to be proclaimed to the church. There are distinctive theological differences in the starting-point between various preachers. One preacher comes to scripture believing that all scripture is authoritative, each jot and tittle requiring meaning for today. The result is an interpretation seeking propositional "truths" or, in difficult passages, resorting to allegorizing. Another preacher may believe that the scripture contains diverse quality, some of it worthy of proclamation but other portions morally inadequate, remnants of primitive cultures unacceptable to the modern world. The result is a truncated canon purged of all offenses to our modern sensibilities. Still another may see the scripture as Word of God valid when it witnesses to the mighty acts of God. The result is a search in the passage for testimony to the redemptive act of God.[11]

The interpreter in the community of faith, called to witness, does not stand at some neutral point. At the starting-point of interpretation there is a commitment, a presupposition of what scripture is intended to be in the community of faith. There is a critical hermeneutical principle at work at the initial starting-point, and the stance of the interpreter determines in large measure the results. The presupposition here relative to scripture issues out in the power of proclamation. Certainly it was the clear commitment of the Reformers to the meaning and place of scripture which made their preaching and interpretations the heart of the Reformation and a model of Protestantism. They came to the scripture with the "hermeneutical principle" that the Bible was the witness to the one purpose of God with his people and that all parts of it were to be read in the light of its center and principle subject: God acting in judgment and mercy in Christ.

Now clearly the challenge for the preacher sitting before a passage of scripture, and for those who would teach the preacher, is for a greater emphasis to be placed upon the central importance of the theological stance at the starting-point. One suspects that a number of sermons are rendered ineffective precisely here. The preacher may have mastered exegetical procedures adequately, but he or she has not come to terms with the faith commitment of what scripture is in the community of faith. Clarity of the hermeneutical process is mandatory at this point. It means for the preacher an examination of his or her faith with a recognition that the material there on the study desk is written in faith and that the greatest organ of under- standing is to listen in expectant faith.

The preacher brings to the interpretive process certain presup- positions, antecedent logical conditions, profoundly affecting his or her work. The position of this paper is that the central and most serious presupposition influencing hermeneutics is one's "doctrine of scripture." This, present at the starting-point, predetermines significantly all that follows. It is the way we start that determines the finish.

That other theological presuppositions are present is self- evident. Lutheran law and gospel, Presbyterian sovereignty of God, Roman Catholic ecclesiology, Pentecostal work of the Holy Spirit—each affects the hermeneutical process. The interpreter comes to a passage with his or her variety of theological baggage, and needs to be aware of its presence and be disciplined lest it usurp and/or distort the basic intention of the passage. Not every biblical passage affirms law and gospel or the work of the Holy Spirit or the triumphalism of the church. It is imperative that we know ourselves and our peculiar theological presupposition.

But the preacher brings to the interpretive process not just pre- suppositions but ideologies, "patterns of beliefs which purport to explain complex social phenomena with a view to directing and simplifying sociopolitical choices facing individuals and groups."[12]

One of the ironies of exegetical work has been the insistence that to do correct exegesis one simply needed to be rid of any dogm- atic theological presuppositions. The great threat to objective study was theological commitments. Overlooked was the fact that other philosophies, concepts, and ideas were crowding to get in—to dominate the interpretive process.[13] Apparent today in the preaching of the Word is that the major threat to the sermon is not theological presuppositions but the use of the biblical passage to speak "my" current ideological views on social and political issues. The passage's Word is muted or distorted. What the passage is used to say is what is already assumed by the preacher to be true. The passage becomes in a sense only the preacher's word and lacks now the authority and power of the revealed Word. This distortion of the interpretation of the passage transforms preaching from pro- clamation to propaganda of a current ideology and affects the whole spectrum of the pulpit from the theological right to left. As Leander Keck has identified it:

> Christian preaching becomes propaganda when it adopts the current ideology instead of entering into struggle with it. It becomes propaganda when current myths and assumptions control what is said or not said, whether it be "religious individualism" as the sacred counterpart to the free enterprise system or religious zealotism as the handmaid of radical reconstruction.[14]

Many preachers in the pulpit in the latter part of the twentieth century, who pride themselves on being "biblical preachers," unfortunately fall into the category of being "propagandizers" for a particular ideological viewpoint. The scriptures are supposedly taken seriously, a biblical passage read reverently before proclamation, but throughout it all is not a search for the Word but the Word used as a rationale for what we already affirm.

What, then, is the resolution of this dilemma? We could assume that the answer lies in the power of the preacher to be "objective." But we have seen earlier that this is unlikely, if not impossible, and that concepts and ideas brought from the contemporary may be indispensable in the interpretive process for preaching. An essential factor in interpretation is the intersection of the biblical passage with the contemporary, the point of contact of the meaning and intention of the biblical passage with the preacher and his or her ideologies. Thus it is essential for the preacher to know himself or herself sufficiently to identify ideologies brought to the passage and to have these ideologies enter into debate or dialogue with the passage, with what Karl Barth has described as "the strange new world within the Bible."[15] But the preacher, to guard against the possible distortion of the meaning of the passage by an ideological viewpoint, needs to be on guard when the biblical passage fails to provide tensions or differences of outlook in relation to the value systems and ideologies in his or her culture. In short, a shock is felt in the interacting of our world with "the strange new world within the Bible." If this is absent, the interpreter needs at least to be aware that there exists the potential danger that the passage's meaning is being distorted by previously held ideologies and presuppositions.

This understanding, however, of the passage's potential for upsetting our cherished presuppositions and ideologies is not a hindrance. Rather, it has the potential of bringing to the process a vitality, a spirited dialogue, a zeal in the search for meaning resulting in increased interest for preacher and congregation.

And yet the preacher needs to be especially sensitive to the fact that here we are dealing with a critical area. While acknowledging the inevitable presence of ideologies, one needs to guard carefully lest an ideology become the starting-point or have the ascendancy in the process. An ideology or a "pastoral problem" or a social issue is not the proper starting-point from which one seeks an answer from scripture. Despite the many contributions Harry Emerson Fosdict made to the American pulpit, helping to rescue it from obscurantism and irrelevancy, his contributions were flawed in his insistence that some identified pastoral problem be the starting-point of the sermon. A problem or social issue vexing his congregation was first identified and analyzed; then he moved to the scriptures to find some solution or insight. While Fosdick was commendably motivated by the desire to rescue preaching from irrelevancy and convinced that congregations were singularly disinterested in discovering what happened to the Jebusites, there was and is a dangerous flaw in his procedure. The flaw lies basically in the fact that too often the controlling factor in the interpretive process becomes the contemporary problem or issue defined by the congregation—our analysis of it, our ideas and insights concerning it. Only after this move is made do we turn to scripture, but then scripture is used in far too many cases simply to buttress or give a rationale to what we have already assumed to be true. No longer does scripture have the role of speaking its unique Word to us; scripture becomes a tool in our hands to serve our purposes. Rather than first listening for that word from "the strange world within the Bible" and being obedient to it and guided by it, we make the scripture a propaganda device.

And is it not the case that for Fosdick, as for so many, the approach was determined by a theological presupposition concerning scripture? Fosdick, reacting against a rigid fundamental and a literal authoritative interpretation of scripture, was strongly influenced by nineteenth-century liberalism and the Enlightenment. These significantly affected his use of scripture: "The Bible is a searchlight," he wrote "not so much intended to be looked at as to be thrown upon a shadowed spot."[16]

Central to the interpretive process are the preacher and that preacher's presuppositions and ideology. To understand himself or herself is a prerequisite for responsible interpretation.

V

As the preacher sits before the biblical passage in "this last link but one" of interpretation, there are involved in the process, as we have described it, not just minister and scripture but also congregation. The preacher does not sit alone before the scripture to be preached next Sunday. The congregation is also present. The members of the congregation are there in the minister's initial contact with the passage—peering over the shoulder, jostling the elbow. There is no way they can be shut out, and indeed, to attempt to do so seriously distorts the interpretive process. They provide the context in which interpretation takes place and have a profound influence upon it. Interpreting what the context is makes a great deal of difference to the preacher sitting before a passage. Is interpretation undertaken to produce a dissertation for a Ph.D., or a manuscript to be presented to the Society of Biblical Literature, or a sermon to be proclaimed to the community of faith? Each setting affects the way the passage is approached, the questions we raise, the questions raised by the passage—our confrontation with it and its with us. These are interpretive questions. The preacher in the parish needs to be aware of the unique context in which the task is undertaken. As Jean-Jacques Von Allmen has described it:

> It is in, with and for the Church that the sermon should be prepared. We cannot be alone in the preparation of a sermon; we are in and with the Church, and it is in order to build her up that we are preparing ourselves.[17]

Thus the proper context for the preacher to interpret is within a congregation which provides for him or her a community of faith for an extended time. Any minister who knows the experience of being a peripatetic preacher in a different pulpit each Sunday, interpreting and writing sermons for unknown congregations, recognizes that something essential is missing in the process. Any professor of homiletics knows that one of the innumerable barriers in teaching homiletics effectively is that the student often is asked to move from biblical passage to sermon with no concrete congregation in mind. Something essential is missing in both listening to and hearing the Word when the preacher lives apart from and uncommitted to a particular community of faith. The resulting sermon, for both peripatetic preacher and seminary student, is something more akin to a lecture than a sermon, an imparting of facts about a passage rather than word formed in dialogue with a known community of faith. "We cannot be alone in the preparation of a sermon; we are in and with the Church." Furthermore, the preacher who sees the task of interpretation as a collegiality between preacher and congregation aligns himself or herself with the congregation before the passage. The preacher is in the same position as the congregation, open to the judgment and the grace of the passage.

But if indeed interpretation involves congregation, the question then is how this is to be accomplished. Ideally, if impractically, this would mean the literal participation of members of the congregation in the interpretive process. Some preachers and congregations have undertaken this. For example, members of the congregations are invited to participate with the minister in a study of the biblical passage a week or so before the preaching event. Both preacher and members of congregation sit before the passage, study it together, listening for the Word. Both preacher and parishioners repond to the passage, raising questions of lack of understanding, indicating what they hear the passage say to them, indicating areas of affirmation or disagreement. The dialogue of the community of faith and the biblical passage actually occurs. The preacher, though a participant, also is "recorder," observing how the passage is heard by the community of faith. Their insights, contributions, and their interpretation become a part of the formation of the sermon. They provide, in a living reality, the "now" of interpretation.

While this method of involvement of the congregation is effective, it is often impractical and has the recognizable flaw of being limited in representing the wide diversities within a congregation What ultimately is the prerequisite of this interpretive mode is for the preacher to exercise pastoral care and to enter into the congregation and know its members so that their lives become part of his or hers. Thus during the process of interpretation they are present in imagination. There sitting at the study desk is the young man on the periphery of faith; there a married couple sitting side by side but separated by unseen barriers tearing apart their marriage; there a woman whose days are marred by loneliness; there an elderly man seeking some sense in the nonsense of the contemporary social scene; there a man who the past week has been told there is no longer any use for him in the business to which he has devoted his life. There they all are, waiting to hear a word that may speak to some of the heavy burdens they bear. P. T. Forsyth speaks of how this pastoral concern affects interpretation:

> I could not treat the matter as an academic quest. I was kept close to practical conditions. I was in a relation of life, duty and responsibility for others. I could not contemplate conclusions without asking how they would affect these people,

and my word to them, in doubt, death, grief, or
repentance.[18]

To be able to do this demands faithfulness of the preacher in the
pastoral role. It is in the daily walk and visitation with parishioners,
identifying where they are, that the preacher enables them to participate in the interpretation of the passage.

This necessity of faithfulness to the pastoral role calls into
question the concept of specialization in ministry. In a multi-staff
church, the "senior minister" may at times delegate pastoral visitation and care to other members of the staff and see himself or herself
as "the preacher." One can understand the pressures of the larger
church necessitating the addition of extra staff, but the preacher
needs to be conscious that detachment from the congregation profoundly affects the hearing of the Word in ministering to the congregation. Dedication and commitment to the congregation as their
pastor is an essential dimension of this "last link but one" in the interpretive process.

VI

The "next to the last link" in the hermeneutical chain deserves
increasing attention. Unexamined critically, it provides the occasion at the least for a weakening of the interpretive process, and
most seriously may provide for serious distortions of the biblical
passages. More work is needed by all involved in this endeavor to
distinguish between preaching as propaganda and preaching as
proclamation of the gospel. Identified by an increasing number of
biblical scholars as of highest priority, the challenge is for an
unceasing conversation between interpretation and theology. One
hopes for evidences of its fruitfulness in the years ahead.

Notes

1. Cf. *The Biblical Interpreter* (Philadelphia: Fortress Press, 1978), pp. 103-114.

2. Clyde Fant, *Bonhoeffer: Worldly Preaching* (Nashville: Thomas Nelson, 1975),
p. 126.

3. I recorded this statement in reading Barth some years ago, and cannot now
locate the exact source, but believe it to be in his *Church Dogmatics.*

4. "Exegesis as a Theological Discipline, "Inaugural Address delivered in Schauffler Hall, Union Theological Seminary, Richmond, Virginia, April 20, 1960, pp. 10-11.

5.   Resources abound describing exegetical procedures. This particular "thumbnail" description is from John Bright, *The Authority of the Old Testament* (Grand Rapids: Baker Book House, 1975), p. 69.

6.   A glaring but deliberate omission is evident in this analysis. To probe into the area of preacher before Word in a search for meaning ultimately involves the work of the Holy Spirit. The inward work of the Holy Spirit bearing witness by and with the Word in our hearts is critical in all interpretive work in the community of faith. This subject, however, transcends the scope of this paper and perhaps defies any critical analysis.

7.   Cf. Leander Keck and G.M. Tucker, "Exegesis," *The Interpreter's Dictionary of the Bible*, Supplementary Volume, (New York and Nashville: The Abindon Press, 1976), pp. 296-303.

8.   *Op. cit.*, p. 23.

9.   *Webster's New International Dictionary*, second edition (1937), s.v. "presupposition."

10.   Cf. Brevard Childs, "Interpretation in Faith: The Theological Responsibility of an O.T. Commentary," *Interpretation* XVIII (October, 1964), p. 437.

11.   Cf. Ernest Best, *From Text to Sermon* (Atlanta: John Knox Press, 1978), pp. 11-12.

12.   *International Encyclopedia of the Social Sciences*, David L. Sills, editor, Volume 7 (New York: The MacMillan Co., 1968), s.v. "Ideology and the Social System," pp. 76-85.

13.   See in relation to this Karl Barth's analysis in *Church Dogmatics*, I/2 (Edinburgh: T. & T. Clark, 1956), pp. 728ff.

14.   *A Future for the Historical Jesus* (Nashville: Abingdon Press, 1971), p. 104. This portion of the paper is strongly influenced by Keck's treatment in the cited work. See also his article "Listening To and Listening For," *Interpretation* XXVII (April 1973), pp. 184-202.

15.   *The Word of God and the Word of Man* (Boston: The Pilgrim Press, 1928), p. 28.

16.   "What is Wrong with Preaching?" *Harper's Magazine* (July, 1928). pp. 133-141.

17.   *Preaching and Congregation* (Richmond: John Knox Press, 1962), p. 49.

18.   *Positive Preaching and the Modern Mind* (Grand Rapids: William B. Eerdmans, 1964), pp. 281-282.

THE SOVEREIGNTY OF GOD

by Patrick D. Miller, Jr.

In his *Introduction to the Reformed Tradition*, John Leith says that popular estimates of the Reformed tradition identifying it with an emphasis on the sovereignty of God have a good basis in fact: "A case can be made that the central theme of Calvinist theology, which holds it all together, is the conviction that every human being has every moment to do with the living God."[1]   A recent Reformed confession reflects that emphasis in its opening paragraph under the rubric, "The Living God":

WE BELIEVE IN GOD,
> We acknowledge one God alone,
> whose demands on us are absolute,
> whose help for us is sufficient.
> That One is the Lord,
> whom we worship, serve, and trust.[2]

It is no coincidence that this theological and ecclesial tradition values the Old Testament on a level with the New Testament, for the same conviction of the majesty and sovereignty of God in and over all is a basic theme of the Old Testament, if indeed not *the* basic theme. In his *Old Testament Theology*, Ludwig Köhler claims that the one fundamental statement in the theology of the Old Testament is this: "God is the Ruling Lord. Everything else derives from it. Everything else leans upon it. Everything else can be understood with reference to it. Everything else subordinates itself to it."[3]

To the extent that the theme of God as Sovereign or Lord is the foundation stone of both Old Testament and Reformed theology, it is appropriate in this volume honoring a distinguished Old Testament and Reformed theologian to lift it up for some analysis and reflection. I do so by identifying three primary images that are vehicles for portraying the sovereignty of God—God as King, Judge, and Warrior—and then suggesting how some basic features of Israel's religious tradition, specifically the conception of the divine assembly, kingship, and prophecy are related to these controlling images.

God the King

The image or theme of God as king is a persistent feature of biblical religion, and thus of biblical theology, from the earliest poetry of Israel, which declares, "The Lord will reign forever and ever" (Exod. 15:18; cf. Deut. 33:4-5; Num. 23:21; Ps. 68:24), to the final visions in the Apocalypse of God on the throne and the multitudes shouting, "Hallelujah. For the Lord our God the Almighty reigns!" (Rev. 19:6).

When we speak of the kingship of Yahweh in the Old Testament, we need to recognize that "king" as divine title originally meant "one god as ruler over other gods." That was true in Ugarit, Mesopotamia and Egypt. In the Israelite worship of Yahweh, this mythological conception was taken over (for example, Pss. 95:3; 96:4; 97:7,9). It had its roots in the mythological pattern discerned in such texts as the Babylonian Creation Epic (*Enuma elish*) in Mesopotamia and the Baal-Anat cycle at Ugarit, in which the god fought against hostile and chaotic forces, achieved victory, and was rewarded with the building of a house (temple/palace) as an eternal abode. The victory also brought about the declaration of the god's eternal rule or kingship.

This pattern had its impact on Israelite conceptions of Yahweh's nature and role but with significant modifications. The rule of God was seen and explicated primarily in terms of human communities, although the cosmic rule of Yahweh was always affirmed. The victory of Yahweh to bring about this divine rule took place primarily over the human forces of chaos (for example, the Exodus story, which culminates in the hymn of Exodus 15, or the stories of conquest and settlement in Joshua and Judges) although this might include victory over the deity who led those opposing forces (as, for example, in I Sam 5:15).[4] The divine rule also came to be extended temporally and spatially without any limits and was understood to have its full manifestation in the future when victory over the hostile nations would be complete and all would acknowledge the universal reign of Yahweh.

As is true generally of the notion of God's sovereignty, the basic features expressed in the image of king are that of *power* and *rule*, the former having to do with the *control* of nature and history, the latter having to do with their *ordering* and *governing*. The power of the Great King is for the sake of rule, but that rule is meaningless and moot without the manifestation of power.

The meaning and force of this theme remains the same throughout the Bible though the definition of the power of this King is always being opened up so that the scepter of authority is often seen to be a shepherd's staff (Ps. 23; Ezek. 34:11-16) as well as a mace—as was true elsewhere in the ancient world—reminding us that the power of the king to subdue enemies is exercised also and ultimately for the protection and care of subjects (note the coming together of warrior, king, and shepherd images in a single portrait of Yahweh in Isa. 40:9-11). In the New Testament, the royal crown is seen to be made of thorns as well as gold, and the laughter of the monarch who in Psalm 2 derides all enemies and sets the chosen human king on a throne has the shape of tears as the throne becomes a cross and the power over all enemies is manifest in a suffering love that is willing to take all their attacks.

God the Judge

To speak of God as judge, as the Old Testament frequently does in ancient confessional statements (Exod. 34:6-7; Num. 14:18-19), story (Gen. 18), song (Pss. 96-99), and prophetic oracle (for example, Amos 4:1-3; 5:7,10-11) and vision report (for example, Amos 7:4-6), is to speak of the Lord as one who judges between right and wrong and rules in favor of the former and against the latter. That ruling, however, is not a passive matter. Again, the imagery of God as judge has to do with power but power in behalf of justice. The theological image reflects the biblical understanding of God's passionate concern for vindication of the right and innocent and punishment of the wicked and guilty, God's continuing desire that right be done in heaven and on earth. The metaphor of God the Judge is the Old Testament's way of saying that there is an ethical grounding of reality and that history and the cosmos embody a moral accountability (for example, Gen. 18:25; Exod. 22:25-27). There are several specific features of this metaphor for the moral:

1. The moral accountability of history will in the end be the vindication of the right. That is what the notion of the vengeance of God is all about, and it is one meaning of the gospel. The vision of the mountain of the Lord in Isaiah 2:1-4 declares Yahweh's future act of judging between the nations and sets that in the context of God's transforming Zion into the city of righteousness and justice. The final judgment visions of the Apocalypse, bizarre though they may be, make the same claim.

2. The judgment of this God is not *dis*passionate, but passionate and *com*passionate.

3 . It is very much the image of God as judge that is in mind as the grounding of the cry of the oppressed individual and the victim, especially in the Psalms, but elsewhere also.

Both of these last two points are well illustrated by one of the case laws in the Book of the Covenant:

> If you lend money to any of my people
> with you who is poor, you shall not be to him as a
> creditor, and you shall not exact interest from him. If
> ever you take your neighbor's garment in pledge, you
> shall restore it to him before the sun goes down; for
> that is his only covering, it is his mantle for his body;
> in what else shall he sleep? And if he cries to me, I
> will hear for I am compassionate (cf. Exod. 22;21-24).

One can see fairly easily the clear relationship of God as judge to the notion of God as ruler or king, for it is always the responsibility of the king to judge between right and wrong and to work in behalf of the right. The interrelationship between king and judge is seen in a number of ways on the human plane and the divine plane:

1. Verbs and nouns for judging/judge are interchangeable with, parallel with, or collocated with those for ruling and ruler.

2 . Numerous texts in the Old Testament and the ancient Near East testify to the judicial role of the king as the determining factor as to whether any king's reign shall continue. Examples:

   a. In the legend of Aqhat from Ugarit, the one royal activity that is depicted of the king Danel is judging the case of the widow and orphan.
   b. In the Kirta epic from Ugarit, the king's son, Yassib, claims that Kirta should give up the throne because of his inabilty to settle the cases of the widow and orphan on account of his illness.
   c. Absalom steals the heart of Israel from David by promising to judge the cases that people are trying unsuccessfully to bring before the king for judgment (II Sam. 15:1-6).
   d. One of the classic statements of the ideal of kingship in the Old Testament is that found in

Psalm 72 where the judicial reponsibility of the king is lifted up (see vss. 1-4 and 12-14).

3 . The Enthronement Psalms, which are among the primary declarations of Yahweh's kingship, couch that reign or dominion frequently in judging language, for example Psalms 96:10-13; 98:7-9; 99:4.

4 . That the imagery of the Lord as judge has a cosmic dimension and has to do with cosmic accountability for the right and for justice in the divine as well as the human realm is well illustrated in Psalm 82.

God the Warrior

With the imagery of God as warrior, we encounter again a pervasive metaphor running through Scripture early and late, Old Testament and New Testament.[5] From the Exodus story to the Apocalypse, the combat of the Lord against opposing forces is a dominant reality. That is inevitably the case in light of the roots of Israel's notion of God in the ancient Near East and its mythology. The warrior image is also inescapably a part of Israel's discernment of God in light of the historical context of Israel's existence and Israel's conviction that history was shaped by and controlled by the Lord.

If the imagery of God as king points especially to the Lord's *rule* of history and the picture of God as judge underscores the *moral* character of history as shaped and directed by this God, the image of God as warrior confirms the *power* of this God that lets us know who indeed is Lord of heaven and earth, nature and history, cosmic and human affairs. The communal, corporate, public, historical character of Israel's life and God's involvement with that life makes unavoidable the claim of God's power in, over, and through the historical vicissitudes of that life. If the New Testament seems to paint God's picture in another way, it is probably because we understand the redemptive and historical work of God in Jesus Christ in highly individualistic terms, which the New Testament often allows us to do or encourages us to do; but that happens also because we ignore both what the New Testament says about the centrality of the *kingdom* of God, the dominion of God—a highly corporate, spatial metaphor shaped by its Old Testament origins—as well as the clear sense in which Paul and others develop a notion of *Christus victor* as an appropriate way of understanding the atonement, God's victory in Christ over all the powers and principalities that oppose the rule of God. The Cross in that sense is the stamp of finality on the Exodus and God's victory over the principalities and powers of Egypt. The struggle goes on, but both the *purpose* of God the Warrior to bring a *basileia* of *dikaiosunē* and *eirēnē*, a kingdom of *sedeq* and *šālôm*, righteousness and peace, into reality and the *power* of God the Warrior to pull it off are demonstrated in the Exodus-Christ axis, which tells us what both history and God are about.

One cannot, therefore, claim history—in the largest sense—as the context and matrix for God's redemptive work or recognize the totality of that as the activity of God without some sense of God's involvement in, through, and alongside—whatever may be the appropriate way of expressing the mystery of God's impingement on the world—the conflicts among people and nations, enhancing, luring, creating, controlling history toward the way that God has set. One way in which Israel spoke about all of that less abstractly and more poetically and doxologically was to sing:

> Yahweh is a man of war,
>> Yahweh is his name (Exod. 15:3).

and

> His right hand and his holy arm
>> have gotten him victory (Ps. 98:1).

Another way in which Israel expressed the convictions described above less abstractly and more dynamically was to tell the story in prose and poetry of how the Lord defeated Pharaoh at the sea. And eventually Israel has to tell stories about the march of God's armies against God's own people for the sake of God's way in the world.

Once again, we need to recognize the dynamic interaction of this image with those of God as king and judge. That is illustrated clearly in a hymn such as Psalm 98:1-3:

> O sing to the Lord a new song,
>> for he has done marvelous things!
> his right hand and his holy arm
>> have gotten him victory.
> The Lord has made known his victory,
>> he has revealed his vindication
>>> in the sight of the nations.
> He has remembered his steadfast
>> love and faithfulness
>>> to the house of Israel.

> All the ends of the earth have seen
>> the victory of our God.

One could add to this Psalm 24 and many other texts. In mythic and historical patterns, kingship is rooted in the power demonstrated in victory over enemies.

That victory, however, is against chaos and oppression. It is for justice and order. It is the victory of the righteous judge and the just king. One sees the interconnection of God as warrior and judge, for example, in Deuteronomy 9:1-6, where the conflict between the Israelites and Canaanites is set in juridical terms, Yahweh indicating by victory over the Canaanites a divine judgment against them. Moses, of course, in this context is contesting Israel's assumption that Yahweh's victory in their behalf is a judgment that they are righteous and innocent.

Features Related to the Primary Images

These images of God as king, judge, and warrior are the formative theological images for the way in which the Old Testament understands and speaks of the rule of God. As such, they help us place and understand three major aspects of the religious life and thought of ancient Israel: the role of the divine assembly, kingship, and prophecy. Each of the three images grounds and shapes these other features in a particular way.

God as the Great King

The theological image or notion of Yahweh as the Great King is tied to *the role of the divine assembly* as a *royal court*, the entourage of the king, servitors to do the king's bidding and maintain the proper rule of the kingdom as well as to give homage and praise to the one who is the Great King.

One of the texts which depicts the heavenly assembly in this way is Isaiah 6. In Isaiah's vision he sees the Great King sitting on a throne surrounded by the seraphim, members of the royal court. They render praise to Yahweh (vs.30) and perform tasks in the assembly. Indeed Isaiah is sent as an emissary of the royal court. A similar picture is given in I Kings 22:19-22 where again a prophet, Micaiah, has a vision of Yahweh enthroned and surrounded by all the heavenly host. In this case a conversation goes on between the Lord and the divine courtiers, one of whom accepts a commission from the Great King. The vision of Ezekiel 1 belongs also to this category as the prophet sees "the appearance of the likeness of the glory of the Lord" (vs, 28b) enthroned above the "living creatures" (vss. 26-28).

Kingship is related to the image of Yahweh as king in that the Israelite King serves as vassal or agent of the Great King, appointed to carry out the Suzerain's rule. A classic text depicting this is Psalm 2 where Yahweh enthroned in the heavens (vs. 4) appoints by decree a king on Zion as the Lord's anointed to rule in God's behalf over the nations. The royal psalms generally reflect such an understanding of the earthly king, as, for example in Psalm 72 where the prayer is uttered:

> Give the king your judgments, O God,
>   and your righteousness to the royal son,
> May he judge *your* people with righteousness
>   and *your* poor with justice (vss. 1-2).

Universal dominion is besought for the anointed of the Great King (vss. 8-11). Psalm 132 and II Samuel 7 also express in various ways the place of the Israelite king as the chosen ruler in Yahweh's behalf.

The *prophetic function* that grows out of the understanding of Yahweh as king is the role of the *prophet as mediator of the relationship between Yahweh and the human king*, the relationship between divine government and human government. As Frank Cross has suggested: "The figure of Samuel in the Deuteronomistic history provided a paradigm of the prophetic leader."[6] In I Samuel 10, Samuel is the agent of the Lord in designating Saul King, and the same role is played by Samuel in the tradition about the selection of David as king in I Samuel 16. Commensurate with this prophetic function, Samuel also announces Yahweh's rejection of Saul from being king over Israel (I Sam. 15:26).

Other prophetic texts bear witness to the function of the prophet as the one who designates Yahweh's king and announces the word of the divine ruler about and to the human ruler. This is reflected extensively in the activity of the ninth-century prophets in the north, for example, Ahijah's designation of Jeroboam as king over the ten northern tribes (I Kings 11:29-39), Elisha's designation of Hazael king over Syria and Jehu king over Israel (I Kings 8:13; 9:6ff.) and announcement of the divinely appointed tasks to which these kings were set (I Kings 19:17; II Kings 8:12; 9:7-10), and Amos' announcement of Yahweh's word: "I will rise against the house of Jeroboam with the sword" (Amos 7:9). The southern prophets also carry out a similar function vis-a-vis the king as one sees, for example, in Isaiah with Ahaz (Isa. 7) and Jeremiah with Johaiakim (Jer. 36:27-32).

There are obviously *prophetic speech forms* appropriate to this function. While judgment speeches and other types come into play, it is particularly the *royal oracles* that are the vehicle for announcing the appointment of the human king by the Great King. They are spoken in the name of Yahweh the King by the prophet, the Lord's messenger. Examples may be found in Isaiah 9:1-6 and 11:1-9 as well as Jeremiah 23:1-6 and 33:14-22. Even in the postexilic period, royal oracles were proclaimed by the prophets Haggai (2:23) and Zechariah (6:9-13).

God as the Righteous Judge

The notion of Yahweh as Judge carries with it the imagery of *the divine assembly as a judicial court*. This is not explicitly reflected in prophetic texts where the divine assembly is referred to, but it is seen in Psalm 82. There the divine council (*ʿădat ʾēl*) is gathered as a judicial assembly and God (*ĕlōhîm*) stands in the midst of the assembly as judge to announce judgment. The judgment is pronounced against the gods, but it is because they do not maintain justice in the human community.

In like manner *kingship* is a refraction of the divine responsibility for maintaining right (*mišpāṭ* and *ṣedeq*) in the universe. In the human community the king is the final human guarantor of justice. That is reflected in Absalom's wooing Israel away from David by offering to hear the claims of those "who came to the king for judgment" (II Sam. 15:1-6), in the appeal of the woman of Tekoa to David (II Sam. 14:1-24) and Solomon's settlement of the case of the two harlots and the one baby (I Kings 3:16-28), and in the prophet's pretended appeal to the king for judgment in I Kings 20:38-43. That the maintenance of justice is a central function of the king as Yahweh's ruler is also reflected in the royal psalms (for example, Ps. 72) and the summary report of David's reign: "So David reigned over all Israel; and David administered justice and equity to all his people" (II Sam. 8:15).

The associated *function* of the *prophet* as messenger of the Righteous Judge is that of *proclaimer of Yahweh's justice and announcer of Yahweh's judgment for breach of covenant law*.[7] Such announcement could be against the king (and so related to the prophetic function described above), the people, and/or the cult. This prophetic responsibility is widely manifest among the preexilic prophets and represents the mass of their prophecy.

Samuel again is a paradigm figure as he announces to Saul Yahweh's word of judgment. In both of the narrative sources of Samuel (I Sam. 13:13-14; 15:10-35) he is depicted as announcing judgment on Saul (rejection of his kingship) for disobeying the command of Yahweh and violating the laws of Holy War.[8] Many other narrative and prophetic texts reflect a similar role. One can cite as examples Nathan's indictment and announcement of judgment against David for the sins of adultery and murder (II Sam. 11-12); Elijah's pronouncement of Yahweh's judgment on Ahab and Jezebel for violation of the inheritance laws, murder, and—along the way—false witness (I Kings 21:17-24); the judgment announced by an unnamed prophet against the king of Israel for violation of the ḥērem requirement (I Kings 20:35-43); Ahijah's proclamation of judgment upon Jeroboam for violation of the covenant law against idolatry and the worship of other gods; as well as such prophetic oracles as Amos 2:6-8; Micah 3:9-12; and Jeremiah 22:1-8 and 13-19.

The *prophetic speech form* peculiarly appropriate to this function is the *judgment speech* consisting of the messenger formula, an accusation of indictment, and a sentence of judgment.[9] The judgment announced by Elijah against Ahab is a parade example:

> And you shall say to him, "Thus says the Lord: 'Have you killed, and also taken possession?'" And you shall say to him, "Thus says the Lord: 'In the place where the dogs licked up the blood of Naboth shall dogs lick your own blood'" (I Kings 21:19).

Most of the oracles of Amos, Micah 1-3, as well as numerous oracles of Isaiah and Jeremiah are of this sort. Other speech forms, however, come into play in this context; for example the covenant lawsuit (Isa. 2:1-3, 18-20; 3:13-15; Mic. 6:1-5), woe oracles forming the indictment in a judgment speech (Amos 5:7, 10-11 [reading *hoy* at the beginning of vs. 7]; 6:1-7; Isa. 10:1-19); lament (Amos 5:1-3); and parable (Isa. 5:1-5).

God as the Warrior Commander

The widespread imagery of Yahweh as warrior has as its central feature the notion of God as commander of the forces of heaven and earth. The *role of the heavenly assembly*, therefore, is that of a *divine army* led by Yahweh. Many texts attest to this military imagery. An excellent example is found in Deuteronomy 33:2-3:

Yahweh from Sinai came
He beamed forth form Seir upon us.
He shone from Mount Paran.

With him were myriads of holy ones
At his right hand marched the divine ones
Yea, the purified of the peoples.[10]

Or Psalms 68:18:

The chariots of God were two myriads,
A thousand the warriors/archers of the Lord,
When he came from Sinai with the holy ones.[11]

One could add the pictures in Judges 5:20, Joshua 10:12-13,[12] and Habakkuk 3 of the cosmic elements aiding Yahweh in battle and the call of the *mal'āk yhwh* to the heavenly assembly to curse the inhabitants of Meroz for not coming to the aid of Yahweh in battle (Jud. 5:23).[13]

The prose literature of the Old Testament refers several times to the march of Yahweh and the divine army (for example, II Sam. 5:22-29; II Kings 6:15-19; 7:6). The most explicit reference is the fragmentary piece in Joshua 5:13-15 where just before the march of conquest begins Joshua meets a man who identifies himself as "the commander of the army of the Lord." The allusion is unmistakably to the heavenly army of Yahweh. Joshua is commander of the Israelite army. The presence of this figure from the divine assembly is an indication that Yahweh and the divine army would march with and assist Israel's army in the battle ahead.

The *role of the king* as the agent of the Divine Warrior is obvious. He is the leader of the human forces in battle. Not only do many narratives of the books of Samuel and Kings bear witness to this function, but such royal psalms as 18, 20, and 21 testify to the centrality of the military role in the ideology of kingship. Indeed that is characteristic of kingship generally. In Israel it is specifically at the command and direction of Yahweh that the king marches. II Samuel 5:22-25 is instructive in this regard. David does not go up into battle without first inquiring of Yahweh what he should do (cf. vs. 19). He is told to attack from the rear, and "when you hear the sound of marching in the tops of the balsam trees, then bestir yourself, for then the Lord has gone out before you to smite the army of the Philistines" (vs. 24). The marching is that of Yahweh and the heavenly army to assist David in battle.

The *prophetic function* associated with the imagery of God as the Warrior Commander is that of herald and interpreter of Yahweh's interventions in war. The prophet is the proclaimer of Yahweh's war.[14] As a kind of prophetic paradigm, Samuel embodies this function also (I Sam. 15:1-35; 28:8-25). The war of Yahweh is not always victory for Israel. Sometimes it is against Israel as in the case of I Samuel 28:17-19 or I Samuel 4-6, where Yahweh delivers Israel into the hand of the Philistines and then defeats the Philistine god, Dagon, and the Philistine army.

The ninth-century prophets carry out this function extensively. I Kings 22 illustrates the case well. Both the four hundred prophets headed by Zedekiah, as well as Micaiah, announce Yahweh's war to the kings. In I Kings 20:13 and 28 unnamed prophets declare to Ahab that Yahweh has given the Syrian army into his hand. Elijah and Elisha are given the rubric "the chariots of Israel and its horsemen" (II Kings 2:12; 13:14), and Elisha is depicted in a series of legendary stories as defeating the Syrian army with the help of the heavenly army (II Kings 6:8-23 [see v. 17] and 6:24-7:20 [see v. 6]).

In classical prophecy of the eighth century and later, the prophets also announced Yahweh's war against an enemy or against Israel/Judah. Amos 1:2-2:6 is a cycle of war oracles that culminates in an announcement of Yahweh's war against Israel (2:13-16). The Day of Yahweh oracle in Amos 5:18-20, by a series of devices—disputation, contrast, simile—declares in an implicit fashion Yahweh's turning now to march against Israel. The prophetic oracles against the nations are a prime example of this function as well as the *speech forms* appropriate to the announcement of Yahweh's war. The doom oracle against Babylon in Isaiah 13:1-22 depicts Yahweh mustering his heavenly and earthly armies to do battle against Babylon. Hosea 5:8ff., Obadiah 15-18; and Joel 4:9ff. (Eng. Joel 3:9ff.) are prophetic oracles announcing Yahweh's war against various enemies. In these texts as well as in the concluding chapters of Jeremiah (46-51) there are numerous examples of the typical oracles of call to battle (for example, Jer. 5:10-11; 6:4-6; 46:3-6, 9-10; 49:14-16, 28-29, 31-33; 50:14-16, 21-23, 26-27, 29-30; Hos. 5:8-9; Joel 4:9ff., and Obadiah 1) and call to flight (for example Jer. 6:1; 48:6-8, 28; 49:8, 30; 50:8-10; Zech. 2:10-13), which declare Yahweh's war and call for an appropriate response.[15]

A word should be said about the prophecy of Deutero-Isaiah, for there we seem to have something quite different from what has been described above. That is less the case than appears, however. The call of the prophet in the context of the decree of Yahweh in the heavenly assembly is present in Isaiah 40:1-11.[16] Yahweh's action as king, judge, and warrior stands behind this call and prophecy. The announcement or message now is of salvation and deliverance rather than judgment. That is the decree of the divine King and Warrior (40:9-11). As judge, Yahweh calls the other gods into court (not in a criminal case, but in a civil suit) to determine and judge that they are powerless and the Lord rules (41:1-5, 21-29). Further, the prophet announces Yahweh's war against Babylon (chap. 47), and continues the imagery of Yahweh as warrior and commander of the heavenly hosts (40:26; 45:12; 51:9ff.; 52:7ff.). With the changed message, come now the speech forms that are characteritic of this prophet, the oracle of salvation (for example 41:8-13) and the proclamation of salvation (for example, 41:17-20).[17]

Concluding Reflections

What we see, then, in this construction is the way in which the images of God as king, judge, and warrior are the grounding of primary institutions and modes of speech in the history of Israel and its religion. These metaphors are not simply interesting ways of imagining God. They are controlling symbols that shape Israel's life and are the conceptual grounding for the *politics of God*. Indeed what we have in this paradigm of God as lord is a view of the *divine government* as it was focused in the nation Israel and a demonstration of the fact that the God of the Old Testament is to be understood in political terms, that is as one who has to do with the affairs of the human world and the divine world, who is seen as the creator and guarantor of order and control in the universe (the Great King), the one whose power in and over the affairs of humanity and the gods effects that control (the Warrior Commander) and the moral ground of history and its end (the Righteous Judge). To translate once again from the dynamic into the abstract, it is *power in behalf of just rule* that Israel saw in its God and that God asserted in Israel's history and institutions (cf. Isa. 2:1-4/Mic. 4:1-4).

The mythopoeic conception of the heavenly assembly, the divine council, is the Bible's way of pointing to a transcendent ordering and governing of the universe, of which all human governments and institutions are a reflection, but even more it is the machinery by which the just rule of God is effective, that is, powerful, in the universe. The divine council gives political shape to the reality of God. Whatever is said about God's power, unity, character, and purpose in some fashion is to be understood in political and social terms, whether one is speaking of God's "being" or God's "activity." The images of God as king, judge, and warrior are not, therefore, individualistic images but social metaphors in that they are tied to conceptions of the divine assembly.

The central human figure in the divine government is the king. This is the one who is given power to effect just or righteous rule in the world. That the king's rule is in behalf of a *just ordering* is seen in such royal psalms as Psalms 72 and 101 and such royal oracles as Isaiah 11:1-9; Jeremiah 22:1-8. That such rule has the whole world in view—against the apparently limited sway of Israel's monarchs—is seen in Psalm 2 where all the kings and nations of the earth are given as a heritage to Yahweh's king on Zion. It is worth noting that the imagery of Yahweh as king predates Israel's own experience with human kingship and that the human king as the centerpiece of the divine government on earth continues long after Israel's own government was no longer under kings. Perhaps more important is that the term that is the primary identification of the human ruler as Israel moves into the future is not *melek* = king, but *mesiâh* = anointed, which is a way of indicating that no particular political form is the vehicle for the divine government on earth but that the critical feature of any political structure that effects the politics of God is that it is "anointed," chosen and representative of God.

The divine government like any good government has some system of checks and balances. The check and balance in this system was (and is?) prophecy. It arose with kingship, which could be the agent of the divine rule or a threat to it. Though the king became God's chosen ruler, the prophet could and did check, counter, chastise, and challenge the king's actions and do so in the name of Yahweh because he or she represented the divine will and rule and asserted the intrinsic relationship between power and justice, government and morality, that was required in Yahweh's kingdom. As messenger from the divine government, the heavenly assembly, (cf. Isa. 6; Jer. 23:17ff.; and I Kings 22) the prophet declares: "Thus says the Lord." Even kings must pay attention and be judged by that word.

To speak, therefore, of God as Lord and to explore that notion in depth *via* the images of king, judge, and warrior is to gain a glimpse into the divine government, the political character and purpose of the Lord of Israel. These images and their significance do not disappear with the closing of the Old Testament, nor should we forget two decisions made by the early Christian community insuring that what Israel had learned about God would continue in that community also.:

a) It read as its Old Testament the Greek translation, in which the name of God is translated as *kurios*, Lord, thus naming God as the power to effect just rule, indicating this is who and what God is.

b) It claimed as the basic confession of the Christian community: *Iēsous Kurios*, Jesus is Lord, a claim that both served to identify Jesus with the *kurios* of the Old Testament and to identify for us the *locus* of God's rule.

For those of us who see God's redemptive way primarily in personal and individual terms, that is, the saving grace that redeems individual existence, the Old Testament asserts a vision of God in highly political terms, breaking open our restriction of the activity and purpose of God to an existential or individual concern. For those of us, however, who look for God's redemptive way in the political affairs of people and nations, that is, the establishment of the kingdom of God through the just rule of human rulers and nations, the Christian confession *Iēsous Kurios* really means what it says: *Jesus* is Lord. And the positive confession was and is a negative word about every Caesar, every political form and rule. They are all relativized; none can be equated with the kingdom of God.

NOTES

1. (Atlanta: John Knox Press, 1977), p. 68.

2. From "A Declaration of Faith," a confession of faith adopted by the General Assembly of the Presbyterian Church in the United States in 1976.

3. (Philadelphia: Westminster Press, 1957), p. 30.

4. Cf. P.D. Miller, Jr. and J.J.M. Roberts, *The Hand of the Lord: A Re-assessment of the "Ark Narrative" of I Samuel* (Baltimore: The Johns Hopkins Press, 1977).

5. Cf. P.D. Miller, "God the Warrior," *Interpretation*, 19 (1965), pp. 39-46; and *The Divine Warrior in Early Israel* (Cambridge: Harvard University Press, 1973).

6. *Canaanite Myth and Hebrew Epic* (Cambridge: Harvard University Press, 1973), p. 223. The treatment of prophecy in this essay is directly indebted to Cross's analysis in chapter 9 of this book.

7. *Ibid.*, p. 224.

8. *Ibid.*,

9. Cf. C. Westermann, *Basic Forms of Prophetic Speech* (Philadelph Westminster Press, 1960).

10. The reconstruction and translation of these verses is that of Cross in *Canaar Myth and Hebrew Epic*, p. 101. For an alternative reconstruction of the difficult next to last line see P.D. Miller, "Two Critical Notes on Psalm 68 and Deuteronomy 33," *HTR*, (1964), pp. 240-43.

11. For discussion of this translation see Miller, *The Divine Warrior in Israel*, 108-09.

12. *Ibid.*, pp. 123-28.

13. *Ibid.*, pp. 99-100.

14. Cf. Cross, *Canaanite Myth*, pp. 223-29; P.D. Miller, "The Divine Council a the Prophetic Call to War," *Vetus Testamentum*, 18 (1968), pp. 100-07.

15. Cf. P.D. Miller, "The Divine Council," *op. cit.*, and R. Bach, *Die Aufforderu zur Flucht un zum Kampf im alttestamentlichen Prophetenspruch* (Neukirchen: Neukirher Verlag, 1962).

16. Cf. F.M. Cross, "The Council of Yahweh in Second Isaiah," *Journal of Ne Eastern Studies*, 12 (1953), pp. 274-77.

17. Cf. C. Westermann, *Isaiah 40-55* (Philadelphia: Westminster Press, 1969).

THE BIBLE AND THE BELIEVING COMMUNITIES

by James A. Sanders

It gives me great pleasure to join with others in this manner to express gratitude to Jim Mays for his years of work as author and editor; the world of biblical scholarship is greatly in his debt.[1]

The need to rethink the relationship between the mainline denominations and the seminaries which serve them is urgent even to the most casual observer on either side of the relationship. James Hopewell has addressed the inadequacy of models followed in those relationships, especially models which view congregations as static constituencies. His was an important contribution to the impetus to rethink the role of the mainline seminary in the complex of American Protestant Christianity in the late twentieth century.

The present essay explores that relationship, focussing on the role of the Bible in congregations and how it is taught in seminary.

The seminaries addressed in what follows are those that consciously understand themselves as serving congregations or communities that view the Enlightenment as a gift of God and a part of *revelatio generalis* — whether all such congregations and their members are fully concious of such a theological position or not. By the Enlightenment I mean not only its intellectual heritage but also its basic characteristic of liberation from all forms of feudalism and the shackles of ignorance, subservience and superstition.

We are not addressing the problems of so-called fundamentalists or any others that understand revelation to have ceased with the Bible or to be limited to hierarchical inspiration, or which do not believe in *revelatio generalis in sensu lato*.

Nor are we addressing humanists or others that understand truth to derive only from inductive search or from human intellectual reflection with no referent beyond it.

Rather we are consciously addressing those who have endeavored to incorporate the Enlightenment into an understanding of the ongoing self-revelation of Reality as rooted in Scripture and tradition; that is those who have endeavored to wed academia, in its broadest and best sense of freedom in the quest for truth, to ecclesia; precisely those who have maintained a hermeneutic of God both as universal continuing creator and as particular continuing redeemer in Israel and in Christ.

Within that broad rubric the present essay addresses more specifically those seminaries whose faculties have come to find their professional and vocational identities more in academia, in its narrower sense, and its guilds than in the believing communities they are designed to serve.

In other words, the seminaries in mind in what follows are those which are a part of secular universities, independent seminaries affiliated with secular universities as well as more distinctly church-related and church-supported seminaries.

In yet other words, the seminaries in mind are those which for the most part have more or less consciously followed the model established by William Rainey Harper in the early years of this century, those "training the scholarly pastor."

The problem addressed, that of the role of the Bible in the ongoing believing communities which find clues to their identity and their life-style through ongoing dialogue with it, is exacerbated in the late twentieth century as much as it was in the late nineteenth century, though in different modes. The so-called modernist-fundamentalist tension was not resolved by either liberalism or neo-orthodoxy. The tension does not dissolve either by focussing almost exclusively on God as creator of all or by focussing almost exlusively on God as redeemer of all through a particular kerygma.

A primary focus of the emerging discipline called canonical criticism is precisely that of the relationship between Scripture and believing community. While it has not yet, to my knowledge, addressed the specific problem of the relationship of mainline seminaries to mainline churches in the late twentieth century, it is undoubtedly time to do so.

The Bible, as canon, comes to us from and through ancient believing communities. Its various parts as well as the whole were formed and shaped principally in the liturgical and instructional programs of the early communities. While most of its literature may have been written by or derived from ancient individuals, nothing in it should be understood to have been contributed directly by an individual without its having been filtered through communities which appreciated it and began the heritage of repetition/recitation which set it upon a tenure track toward canon. One of the major problems in mainline seminary instruction in Bible has been a focus on ancient individuals, either "original" writers or redactors. Redaction criticism has underscored the focus. Canonical criticism provides a corrective in this regard.

The mode of understanding the formation of canon since Johann Salomo Semler and his students toward the end of the eighteenth century has been to see it as principally the final stage in the literary formation of the canon; that is, how the larger literary units, the several books, were decided upon as either in or out of the canon.[2] The only attention paid in that mode to the role of the community was limited to the positing of councils at certain moments which decided such issues; this is now seen as anachronistic in its importing later notions of authoritative consistories which had the power to make such decisions for all the communities. Little attention was apparently paid to the implications of such a view which would have presupposed certain models of inspiration and authority which are now seen as hardly realistic — groups of men (sic) making momentous decisions for all time with their minds shaped and focussed on a limited and particular set of problems and concerns and perceptions of them!

Conjoined in the model was a criterion for inspiration or canonicity stated by the Jewish historian, Josephus — a great name ancient and revered enough to bear authority in the ongoing memory of the community.[3] Recent work on the Semler model has shown that passages in ancient noncanonical literature which fit the model, such as lists of books compiled by well-known individuals, passages mentioning gatherings of leaders, passages which stressed the importance of inspired individuals in antiquity, were those which were cited to describe canonization. The Western scholar's need to envisage the role of individuals in the process gave scholarship the eyes to see such references but blinded it apparently to the common sense needed to perceive the importance of the believing communities in the canonical process. No individual in antiquity, no matter how "inspired," slipped something he or she had written into the canon by a side door! It has all come through the worship and educational programs of ancient believing communities or we would not have it. The newly revised concepts and methods in text criticism have indicated a more realisitic view of what actually happened. The focus must now be on communities and the individuals within them, rather than almost exclusively on individuals. The so-called secondary or spurious passages in the Bible, even those "added by a later hand" are also canonical.

Along with the new realism concerning the formation of canon has come a revised model for understanding the inspiration of

Scripture. Heretofore, whether for literalists or liberals, the model has been that of inspiration of an individual in antiquity whose words were then more or less accurately preserved by disciples, schools and scribes. The only difference between liberals and conservatives in this regard has been quantitative.

The critical search for the *ipsissima verba* of the original speaker or writer has been a major focus of biblical criticism. And that focus is fully justified insofar as the scholar is working in her or his shop as a literary historian. So far as I am concerned it should never stop: the tools for recovering original moments in antiquity are improving constantly and should continue to be developed.[4] But that original moment was only the beginning of a process of transmission which took place not only in preserving "schools" but in ancient believing communities which so believed in the value of the original "moment" that it began a process of re-presentation of relevance to the problems of the ongoing community.

Such early schools engaged as much in the re-presenting process as in the preserving process: the two factors of stability and adaptability emerge as of very real importance in understanding the canonical process as well as in understanding today any valid model of the relationship between Bible and believing community.[5]

The new model for understanding inspiration of Scripture is that of the Holy Spirit at work all along the process of formation of Scripture (of whichever canon of whichever believing community — Jewish, Protestant, Roman, Greek Orthodox all the way to the Ethiopian Orthodox Church) as well as through its textual and versional transmission into the ongoing preserving and representational process. This should and must include Enlightenment modes of study of Scripture, discovery of ancient manuscripts, and recovery of apparently sharper information about ancient historical, political and social contexts and cultures which nurtured the texts at all the layers of its formation.

What emerges from viewing the whole of a community's Bible as canon (again, whichever canon of whichever community) is honesty about its wholeness. In contrast to selecting a canon within the canon on which to base the theological construct of whatever denomination, canonical criticism eschews efforts at either harmonization or reductionism and admits from the outset that like the awe-inspiring Cathedral of Chartres, the Bible as canon is a glorious mess.[6] There can be no avoidance of recognition of its anamolies and discrepancies, that is, of its pluralistic richness. The fact that different generations of even a single believing community have different eyes with which to read it and derive value from it must not blind responsible study of it to its canonical pluralism. Different generations as well as different communities have different needs which permit them to see different values on which to base their self-understanding as well as their world view. This is a part of human humility and limitation so well described in most of its literature.

The most pervasive images that emerge from the canon as a whole, by which believing communities may understand who they are, are those of church and synagogue as pilgrim folk, witnesses, servants, and stewards.

The model for understanding the called people of God which seems most pervasive in Scripture, whether in the Jahvist, the Deuteronomic historians, the Chronicler, the Psalmists, evangelists, Paul or the writer of Hebrews, is that of the pilgrim folk. "We are strangers and sojourners as all our forebears were" David is wont to have prayed (I Chron.29:15). The ongoing dialogue between canon and community is based in large measure on that understanding of identity. As Hopewell apparently saw, the believing community should be perceived in dynamic terms rather than static. Surely such a view is firmly based in this image of understanding the believing community as a pilgrim folk in serious dialogue with Scripture. The image of the church as on a pilgrimage is not the only one discernible in Scripture, but its importance puts it perhaps first in any such list of images.

The called witnesses of God are those who inherit a vision, a peculiar manner of seeing the world and their place and function in it. St. Paul and others called this *phronēsis*, a mind set; others speak of it as vision. St. Luke in two volumes of excellent theological history writing rang in the changes in fugue and counterpoint on God's providing for himself "eyewitnesses and servants of the word" (Luke 1:2) through the generations so there might be a folk to witness to what was Reality and its role in human affairs. The prophets can not be fully understood only as spokespersons and covenant mediators; they were also witnesses to how God was signifying the power-flows in the Iron Age Near East from the middle of the eighth century BCE to the end of the sixth, precisely the time of rise and fall of empires most impinging on the life of Israel, bringing about both its death and its resurrection as Judaism.

Luke's other term, *'upēretai*, means "servants," not "ministers" as the current RSV would have it. This image for understanding the believing community or called folk of God is also pervasive in

Scripture. It ought to rule out all self-serving readings of Scripture but apparently does not when insufficiently stressed. Election is to service not to rewards. Whether the servant be suffering or not, the service centers in being a vehicle for God's blessing all his creatures, all the families of the earth.

A fourth pervasive image for self-understanding of the believing community is that of stewardship. As pilgrims, witnesses and servants we are also stewards of whatever we perceive ourselves to have control of or power over. I actually know some Presbyterians who think they own something in this brief passage from womb to tomb! We are but stewards where power lurks — the body, the mind, the spirit, family, friends, or ought of worldly goods. Idolatry is not only something ancient Canaanites engaged in; it is the persistent temptation of the called people of God, community and individual — loving God's gifts so much that we forget they are gifts, that we let ourselves think we have possession of them.

Finally, the called people of God believe unstintingly that there is a moral dimension to the universe, that there is Integrity to Reality (oneness in God), and that there is and will be accountability. Canonical pluralism does not permit writing a scenario of how that accountability is or will be expressed; but dialogue with Scripture renders belief in it firm and unshakeable.

The ongoing dialogue between canon and community is understood as centering in the two questions dynamically conceived: that of faith and that of obedience — identity and life-style.

The Bible, as canon, may be viewed in essence as the authoritative record of that dialogue as pursued from the inceptions of the believing communities, Jewish and Christian, through to the establishment of what Jacob Neusner calls Formative Judaism, on the one hand, and of the Early Church, on the other. It may be viewed as the received record of the struggles of those early believing communities, through five culture eras, to pursue the Integrity of Reality (Oneness of God). The idioms, mores and customs of those five eras form the expressions of the struggle. The expression includes numerous types of literary genres; but none fails to monotheize. While some portions monotheize more thoroughly than others, or appear to do so, the literature which makes up any of the canons of the believing communities, Jewish and Christian, monotheizes more or less well. It would indeed appear that those portions most embarrassing to the modern or Enlightenment mind are those that monotheized most thoroughly (the hardening of the heart of Pharaoh, the commission to Isaiah, Peter's sermon at Pentecost).

Central to the concept of the Bible as canon is the hermeneutics by which the early communities of faith engaged in the struggle to monotheize. The tools of criticism by which to ferret out those hermeneutics are in hand and improving. There is even the possibility on the horizon that we may need to say that the intrabiblical hermeneutics so recovered may be viewed as being as canonical as the actual texts.

The Bible as canon of the believing communities is the paradigm whereby they may learn how to engage dynamically in the same struggle to monotheize today as our ancestors in the faith did in their time. The first commandment is not simply the first of ten, it is proton in every sense one may imagine. The canon is therefore not to be viewed as a box of ancient jewels still valuable and negotiable, but rather as the paradigm whereby current believing communities may resist polytheizing, or fragmentizing of truth, but rather learn in our several cultural spaces to pursue the Integrity of Reality.

The forms of polytheism rampant today may be more insidious and perhaps less clear than they were in antiquity, but they are just as forceful and pervasive as ever they were. It is perhaps more rampant today because we heirs of Judaism and Christianity think we are monotheists. Christianity is especially vulnerable at this point precisely because of the centrality of the concept of the Incarnation — the most precious and the most dangerous concept in Christianity. We have permitted ourselves to think that our Christ revealed God! We have permitted ourselves to think that our Christ in the Incarnation domesticated God. We have permitted ourselves to think that God is a Christian. Polytheism of various sorts is rampant in the thinking of Christians: the concept of the trinity is usually expressed in polytheistic terms; the concept of the satan, or tester, is usually expressed in polytheistic terms. We permit ourselves in reading the New Testament to identify with Christ and thus entirely miss the blessing of his prophetic and challenging words and life and death and resurrection. We have denigrated Paul's concept of the Christian's being *'en Christō* to the point of identifying with Christ and at best pitying the poor benighted Jews and Romans who rejected him.

A salient function which the Bible as canon can have in the believing communities today is that of a prophetic voice challenging the witnessing, serving stewards of the pilgrim folk to take the next step on the journey begun by Abraham and Sarah. I suggest that hearing the Bible as God's prophetic voice is its most important function in its dialogue with current believing communities.

In order to hear that voice, so necessary to the pilgrimage, we must learn to read the Bible on its own terms, that is, by the canonical hermeneutics embedded in it at all layers of its formation.

To what purpose? To fulfill the vocation of the heirs of Abraham and Sarah, whether by blood or by Christ, of being instruments whereby God may indeed bless all the families of the earth. Current suggestions that incorporate Americanism into Christianity with its idols of success and prosperity need to hear the challenge. I recently saw a bumper sticker stating, "Prosperity is your divine right"! The rampant polytheism in the current electronic church is so patent as to be shocking. The current form of hard-core fundamentalism is perhaps the most idolatrous and polytheistic.

The hermeneutics that emerge from within Scripture itself, both those by which we see community traditions continually represented and those by which we see international wisdom continually adapted, are precisely the monotheizing view of God as both universal creator of all peoples and particular redeemer in Israel and in Christ. But even that redemption must finally be seen in the light of God as universal creator, and God's being creator must finally be seen in the light of God's being redeemer. The final redemption is eschatologically a re-creation.

If the Bible is read with God as primarily redeemer in mind, then it easily is falsified as a text into denominationalism and ultimately a new tribalism. This is Christianity's greatest failing, especially wherever the New Testament is viewed as more authoritative than the Old or whenever Marcionism intrudes.

If the Bible is read with God as universal creator in mind solely, then it easily is falsified as a text into a flaccid kind of universalism which lacks reality.

Recent study of true and false prophecy in the prophetic corpus has shown that the real difference between the so-called true and the so-called false prophets was in their hermeneutics.[7] Falsehood crept in when God was seen only as the peculiar God of Israel, only as Israel's redeemer; there are no instances of God being seen only as universal creator, even in the purely Wisdom literature, and certainly not in the prophetic corpus. But even if one should want to assert that the Wisdom literature fails to ring in the changes on God as redeemer, that literature must be seen as but a part of the canon as a whole.

There clearly are portions of the church or segments of the believing communities which need a reading of Scripture which might be called constitutive or supportive of what they are already thinking and doing or have embarked upon. One thinks of those communities made up of nondominant culture constituencies, minorities, third-world communities under oppression, many of whom are in main-line denominations! One of the evolved or developed hermeneutic visions that emerge from such study of the Bible as here described is that of God's bias for the weak and dispossessed, the powerless, indeed, for the slave people come out of Egypt up to the point of entering into the gifts of the promise and the sin of corruption induced by the power of the blessing.

But the mainline communities described above hardly fit into such a category. Where they might, then adjustment to a constitutive hermeneutic is in order. Nonetheless, for most of those we address in our concern about the relation of seminary to congregation it is a prophetic reading of Scripture which is in order at the community level. At the individual level, as in the case of those who lack power to oppress as community, adjustment in hermeneutic is indicated.

The believing communities which I understand to be in the purview of our study desperately need to learn to read the Bible on its own terms, by the hermeneutics which emerge from the canon itself so that they may hear a prophetic voice that challenges: a) their very concept of God, or Reality; b) for Christians their very concept of Christ; and c) their very concept of church or election. There are surely other challenges that are needed but most certainly are they needed in terms of the actual understanding of Christianity one finds in most mainline churches concerning precisely God, Christ and the church.

My understanding of the Bible as canon, or as the churches' book, has been developed over the past thirty years as much in actual congregations and pastors' groups as in the seminary classroom. What I have arrived at in this regard [8] has been forged over those years on precisely the anvils of mainline seminary curricula and of mainline , white power-centered congregations and judicatories. I have for some fifteen years been an affiliate member under watch-care of a black church in Bedford Stuyvesant (largely to try to maintain some kind of Christian sanity) and preach perhaps twice a year in black pulpits; and some of these experiences are a part of my understanding of canon and community. But there have been the two anvils, not just academia, but also ecclesia of the sort we can experience in this country and to some extent abroad.

It is my conviction, out of these experiences, out of viewing the ancient believing commmunities which bequeathed us these texts we call sacred through what we know of modern believing communities, and out of viewing the latter in the light of what I have assiduously tried to learn about the former, that something like a complete revision of our concepts of seminary and church needs to be attempted.

Hopewell was quite right that those in seminaries need to revise their understanding of congregations. The latter, like ancient Israel and the early church, are continually changing and continually evolving, ever moving from one cultural and political context to another, even though imperceptively perhaps at times. But it is far from certain that those congregations enjoy a self-understanding based on responsible dialogue with Scripture; they certainly do not have a self-conscious identity based on the hermeneutics herein suggested. Hopewell, of course, did not claim they did.

Is it possible for the seminaries so to relate to the communities they serve that they might both understand themselves as a part of one and the same pilgrimage, *in sensu lato*, both needing accurately to hear the Word of God available through a prophetic hermeneutic reading of Scripture? Both? As noted above, the seminaries we serve and address tend to view themselves, through their faculties, as a part of academia more than as a part of ecclesia. Even so, they have a largely static view of seminaryhood. Oh, we all like to say we are constantly learning and hopefully improving but this is said for the most part in terms of our identity in our guilds. Is it possible for the seminaries more faithfully to exhibit a self-understanding that transcends academia, to conduct themselves as though they really believed they were a part of a called community as well as the practitioners of Enlightenment thinking and study?

By the model here espoused the seminaries would attempt to provide through dynamic theologizing and reflection models for hearing the voice of God not only through paradigmatic readings of the Bible but also through paradigmatic readings of Enlightenment culture, taking cues precisely from the biblical authors and contributors both in their re-presenting authoritative community traditions and in their adapting the best of international wisdom to ever-changing contexts.

By this model the seminaries would attempt consciously to show the way for the communities to listen for the dynamic Word which expresses the Integrity of Reality. They would by the same model consciously attempt to show the way to sift through cultural stimuli and adapt new wisdom as a part too of the gifts of God. They would consciously attempt to show the way to search Scripture for the challenge and guidance needed, as well as for the encouragement needed to take another step on the pilgrimage.

Humankind is in A.B. 40, the fortieth year of the bomb. Earth hangs by a thin but firm thread of divine grace. (Surely these forty years are not attributable to human sagacity.) As children of the Enlightenment we live between the pride thereof and the fear of its most imposing product. Hope can be derived only from the belief that there is Integrity to Reality. That belief can be due only to the vision which is the gift of Word and Spirit; we can but grope about it inductively like the three blind persons around the elephant. Final hope is that that Integrity continues to reach out for us to integrate us unto itself and continues to grant us the grace that enables us to pursue that Integrity in our lives. The promise is that some of it may rub off on us as witnessing communities and even as individuals.

To monotheize while reading the Bible in order to hear the prophetic voice the seminaries and communities need to hear can start at the simple point of refusing to read the Bible or history by the hermeneutic of good-guys-bad-guys but to read it by dynamic analogy. American believing communities need to understand that God's hardening the heart of Pharaoh is not all that difficult to understand if we read Exodus identifying with Raamses II and the Egyptians. His argument to Moses was ours: hold on, you're moving too fast! if Pharaoh's heart had been soft, there might be a stele of stones out near Goshen for an archaelogist to dig up honoring Pharaho's emancipation proclamation; but we would have no Torah. That requires theologizing, precisely monotheizing, while reading scripture and not moralizing. Torah, hence gospel, is God's emancipation proclamation for all the world. Just as it was not Pharaoh's proclamation, neither was it intended for Israel or church alone.

Monotheizing while reading the New Testament would mean refusing to identify with Jesus in doing so, but rather seeing ourselves in the Pharisees and the Romans. A theocentric hermeneutic which monotheizes emphasizing God as the universal creator of all peoples, as well as redeemer in Israel and in Christ, would permit us to hear the challenging words of Christ's prophetic ministry and life, and permit us to take the further steps we must on the pilgrimage on which we are embarked. I wager that anti-Semitism, racism, sexism as well as other forms of bigotry would very nearly disappear from the Christian soul if we learned to read the New Testament with the basic hermeneutics by which the New Testament writers read what was Scripture for them up to their time, the Old Testament. But so would our self-serving readings, our tendencies to separatism and exclusivism, and especially our own American forms of hardheartedness as viewed by much of the rest of the world.[9]

Seminaries must learn to practice the paradigm and show the way for the believing communities to pursue the Integrity of Reality, not only in the "training" of their future pastors and other ministers but as paracommunities of faith whose role in the ongoing mutual pilgrimage is in part that of providing a consciously working paradigm for reading Scripture, tradition and the ongoing world in which we live so as to discern the guiding Torah or Word of Reality's Integrity on the pilgrimage.

The seminary as a paracommunity of faith would not be a church any more than a church should try to be a seminary. Their roles would be quite distinct.

The model would not provide the larger community of faith with the answer or Word, but would provide the paradigm for how to see and hear both the ancient struggles to monotheize and the ongoing ever-changing modern struggles to be witnesses to that Integrity which alone claims and redeems humanity.[10]

Notes

1. Mays is also a contributor to canonical criticism; see e.g. "Historical and Canonical: Recent Discussions about the Old Testament and Christian Faith," in *Magnalia Dei: The Mighty Acts of God'. Essays on the Bible and Archaeology in Memory of G. Ernest Wright*, edited by F.M. Cross *et al* (Garden City: Doubleday, 1976), pp. 510-28. Mays is a dedicated churchman as well whose concerns about seminary and church I trust are expressed to some extent in the present essay.

The essay was originally written for the Consultation on the Congregation and Theological Education at the Candler School of Theology, June 3-5, 1985.

James Hopewell's paper, "A Congregational Paradigm for Theological Education," *Theological Education* (Autumn 1984), pp. 60-70, was a point of reference for the Consultation.

2. Cf. Semler, *Abhandlung von freier Untersuchung des Canons* (Halle, 1771-76). For further references see Sanders, "Adaptable for Life: the Nature and Function of Canon," *Magnalia Dei* (above, note I), p.552, n. 2; and Brevard Childs, *Introduction to the Old Testament as Scripture* (Philadelphia: Fortress, 1979), pp. 30-60.

3. *Contra Apionem*, Volume I, pp. 37-46.

4. These same tools are currently being applied to the formation of Qumran

literature with considerable effect in reconstructing the history of the Qumran settlement as related to and distinct from the Essenes. Canonical criticism can be applied only in a limited way to study of the Qumran literature since a) we do not know for sure all they considered canonical, and b) they ceased to exist as a discreet believing community with the destruction of the Qumran settlement. See the recent discussion by Philip R. Davies, "Eschatology at Qumran," *Journal of Biblical Literature* 104 (1985), pp. 39-55. His note 9 on p. 41 is inexact; Davies should not refer there to canonical criticism but to Brevard Childs' work on canonical context.

5. See the discussion in "Adaptable for Life" (above, note. 2).

6. John James, *Chartres: The Masons who Built a Legend* (London: Routledge and Kegan Paul, 1982), p. 9: "When you examine the cathedral closely, you discover to your immense surprise that the design is not a well controlled and harmonious entity, but a mess."

7. Sanders, "Hermeneutics in True and False Prophecy," *Canon and Authority: Essays in Old Testament Religion and Theology* (Philadelphia: Fortress, 1977), pp. 21-41.

8. In *Canon and Community* (Philadelphia: Fortress, 1984) and *From Sacred Story to Sacred Text: Canon as Paradigm* (Philadelphia: Fortress, 1986).

9. See a list of seventeen possible results in Christian congregations if canonical hermeneutics were to be used in them and by their members in reading the Bible, in *Canon and Community* (above, n. 8), pp. 74-76.

10. A full working bibliography on current discussions on canon is included in *From Sacred Story to Sacred Text* (above, n.8).

TRANSLATING, PREACHING AND OUR WORDS FOR GOD
by Paul D. Hanson

One of the results of a fuller participation of women in leadership roles of the church has been a greater sensitivity to the language we use for God and for each other. Though the degree to which this sensitivity has transformed language varies from church to church and region to region, it is increasingly the case that if sermons, prayers and liturgy refer to God exclusively with male pronouns and to humanity with terms like "man," formidable barriers are raised between worship leaders and many members of the congregation.

An historical-linguistic argument is often advanced, to be sure, in defense of such usage. But this approach to the problem is ill-advised for two reasons: 1) It overlooks the organic nature of language, according to which change is inevitable and essential; 2) To insist on traditional usage, regardless of the pain it causes for large numbers of people in the church, violates the highest of all Christian principles, the law of love.

When the issue of language is discussed within the context of a religious community, participants must be aware that they are dealing not with a triviality, but with a substantive matter. For the words we use in naming or referring to God go beyond matters of taste and style to important theological and social questions. For example, we are increasingly aware of the effect that the domination of male images for God within a community has upon the relative positions of males and females within that community. For centuries, women have not enjoyed equal access to positions of leadership within the major Christian confessions, a fact intertwined with the language used for God in Scripture, prayers, preaching and liturgy and with the picture of God as male fostered by such usage. Within denominations committed to replacing patterns of discrimination with equality for all members, regardless of race or gender, the problem of language must be regarded as a major theological problem.

The attitudes adopted in dealing with the problem of language can provide an index for measuring the spiritual health of a community of faith. A healthful response to the problem will be characterized both by a clear awareness that the nature of God transcends distinctions of gender and all other human characteristics, and by a loving sensitivity to the experiences and understandings that underlie the responses of various individuals to the words we use for God. For example, to respond to the pain evoked by the metaphor of God as "Father" within women for whom the metaphor of "Mother" is also precious, or whose experiences of males have been marred by repressive authoritarianism and abuse with stern insistence on the normative status of the male metaphor, is to ignore a profoundly important theological and human problem. On the other hand, where such problems are treated patiently and caringly, tremendous spiritual growth typically occurs, leading to lasting gains. Women discover a language that enhances rather than inhibits a growing relationship with God. Men find that their spiritual understanding is stretched and enriched. Children grow up with a sense of spiritual equality and empowerment of all people, and with a model for addressing problems and differences nondefensively, positively, and without the inclination to diminish the worth of other individuals.

In the experience of my family, it has been heartening to witness the effects of a creative and thoughtful approach to the problem of language on our children. We have been fortunate to belong to a church which over the years has been served by a male/female copastorate, and in which children are valued members. Numerous discussions on various levels have been devoted to the language we use for God and for each other. Opinions have differed greatly, and sometimes tension has reached a high level. But through the process an inclusive form of language has evolved in all aspects of worship, and creative experimentation has gone on in translating the lections. These efforts have not gone unnoticed by the children of the church, and occasionally we are reminded of that fact. For example, our daughter Amy, when she was eight, responded to a reading of I Corinthians 11:2-16 with the firm declaration, "The man who wrote that should have his head soaked in water!" Some months later we observed her busily writing in her bulletin during the sermon, only to find at the end of the service not the usual doodles, but careful editing of the contents in which the vestiges of sex-discriminatory language had been removed. To be sure, the sense of empowerment that such actions foster challenge traditional patterns of authority in unanticipated ways, as illustrated by our Nathaniel, who, shortly after having learned to write, occupied himself during a lengthy sermon filling out a visitor's card. Name, address and phone number were correctly entered (with some help from his older brother, Mark). On the line asking whether pastoral services were desired, he wrote in a bold hand: "I quit church!!"

The above observations obviously are in harmony with the many voices calling for a creative, progressive attitude in the church towards the language we use for God and for each other. Nevertheless, there is a particular point at which I differ with some proponents of creative change, a point having to do specifically with the guidelines set up for translators of the Bible as they deal with the various types of noninclusive language found in the Bible. This issue has been discussed by the Revised Standard Version Committee of the National Council of Churches of Christ in the U.S.A. over the course of its preparation of a new revision of this widely used translation of the Bible. The discussion took on an added intensity in 1980 when a Task Force on Biblical Translation, which had been authorized by the Unit Committee of the Division of Ministry and Education of the National Council of Churches, issued a statement urging the RSV Bible Committee to proceed more boldly in eliminating male-biased language, both in reference to God and humans.

Though the members of the RSV Bible Committee reaffirmed their commitment to eliminate male-biased language introduced through translation but not found in the original languages, and to provide a translation which was as inclusive as possible within the restraints imposed by fidelity to the historical meaning of the original texts, they refused to resort to additional, deletions or changes that were without textual basis, arguing that such exercises belong to the domain of the "targum" or parphrase, and not to responsible translation techniques. By way of example, the King James Version frequently uses "man" or "men" where the original Hebrew or Greek had the equivalent of "any one." To demasculinize the text in such cases is to provide a more accurate translation. The same applies to cases where the Hebrew uses *'ish* and the Greek *anthropos* to refer generically to "people." In proverbial sayings, the Hebrew often contrasts "the wicked" with "the righteous," which though singular in form clearly are collective in meaning. The older translations rendered these in the singular, with the result that the subsequent male pronouns gave such sayings a masculine flavor which was not intrinsic to the original meaning. In such cases, a translator seeking to give an accurate translation which is yet sensitive to the issue of inclusive language is perfectly justified, in my opinion, to treat "the wicked" and "the righteous" as plural, with subsequent neutral plural pronouns.

The case is quite different, however, when one encounters male-dominated language that actually reflects patriarchal attitudes and practices within the social milieu reflected by the biblical text. An example of this is the standard form of ancestral covenantal promise, which is extended to and handed down through the generations by way of the male family heads, which form, though unacceptably limiting against contemporary standards of inclusivity, was an undeniable part of the ancient Israelite milieu (e.g., Deut. 30:20b: "that you may dwell in the land which the Lord swore to your fathers, to Abraham, to Isaac, and to Jacob, to give them"). To alter such a text through the addition of the names of female ancestors, though enhancing inclusiveness in the direction of what is deemed theologically proper within the context of our present understanding of God's will, tends to obscure the texture of the passage's original historical and social setting, and thus goes beyond the limits imposed upon the translator.

Discussions between different groups sponsored by the National Council of Churches clearly indicated that two different approaches to the questions raised by gender-biased language in the Bible were represented respectively by the RSV Bible Committee and those who were pressing for a more bold approach. The result was the authorization by the Unit Committee of the preparation and publication of *An Inclusive-Language Lectionary*, a project to be carried out by an Inclusive-Language Lectionary Committee distinct from the RSV Bible Committee. The first volume, *Readings for Year A*, appeared in 1983, with volumes covering years B and C following in 1984 and 1985.[1] The theological assumptions informing the work of the Inclusive-Language Committee as they come to expression in the Preface of all three volumes can be summarized as follows:

1. All persons are equally loved, judged, and accepted by God.

2. Basic to a sense of equality and inclusiveness in the recognition that God by nature transcends all categories.

3. God's holiness and mystery are present in the biblical tradition even if the words used to describe God reflect limitations—words and language convey as best they can what is virtually impossible to describe.

In addition to these three points, the committee expressed its goal in the following terms: "to create for use in services of worship inclusive-language lectionary readings based on the Revised Standard Version of the Bible, with the text revised only in those places where male-biased or otherwise inappropriately exclusive language could be modified to reflect an inclusiveness of all persons."

I believe that the three theological assumptions formulated in the Preface of the *Inclusive-Language Lectionary* are in harmony with the heart of a biblically-based understanding of the Christian faith. It is interesting to note, moreover, that a distinct tension exists between the first and second points on the one hand, and the third on the other. This is inevitably the result of an essential aspect of the biblical faith, namely, its confession that God's nature and will come to expression within the events that comprise human experience, that is to say, within the historical and socio-political realm. This is a realm within which world views, and the concepts and language-systems related to these world views, both are conditioned by various historical and cultural determinants and are in the process of constant change. It is, therefore, inevitable that the world views of the different periods covered by biblical history are reflected in the writings of the Bible. Far from detracting from the majesty and authoritativenes of the Bible as the Word of God, these historically and culturally determined elements draw attention to the dynamic nature of the revelatory process found in Scripture, and the rootedness of that process in human experience. It makes clear that God has been active in the lives of real humans, who like ourselves, related to God precisely within the limits and the possibilities of their particular time in history.

It is in fact this revelatory process, occurring within the relationship between God and the historical communities spanning the broad sweep of biblical times and extending down to contemporary communities of faith, that provides the historical basis for the Inclusive Language Committee's assumptions that "all persons are equally loved, judged, and accepted by God," and that "God by nature transcends all categories." And it is one of the miracles of faith that such convictions have arisen out of a chain of confessions marked by a high degree of conceptual and linguistic diversity, a diversity giving clear expression to the limitations referred to in the third theological assumption described in the Preface to the Inclusive-Language Lectionary.

At what point, then, do I differ with the approach of the Inclusive-Language Committee? Clearly not in believing that contemporary expressions of faith, whether in prayer, preaching, contemporary confessions, and religious instruction should utilize inclusive language in referring both to God and humans. In all such activities, we should strive toward an inclusiveness which embodies and reflects the fruits of our long and rich confessional heritage. The problem arises rather, in my judgment, in the area of translating the Bible. Specifically as regards the stated intention of the *Inclusive-Language Lectionary*, this problem arises in connection with biblical passages "where male-biased or otherwise inappropriately exclusive language could be modified to reflect an inclusiveness of all persons."

Before turning to this expression of the Committee's goal, I want to make one point regarding the nature of the Lectionary project. I agree with the members of the Inclusive-Language Lectionary that their project is experimental, and subject to further revision. Their experiment, moreover, has been helpful in raising an important problem to a level of consciousness heretofore unknown in the church. It is in the spirit of continued dialogue and experimentation that I now wish to raise a theological point that I feel has not been considered sufficiently by the Lectionary Committee.

The problem hinges on defining what "male-biased or otherwise inappropriately exclusive language" should be removed from a collection of writings which, as we have noted, stems from and reflects many different historical periods and cultures. As we have already noted, instances of such usages which are not rooted in the original languages, but which have been introduced by later translators and often reflect the practices and biases of their times, should be removed. But what of such language when it is rooted in and reflects the practices and biases of the biblical writers themselves?

Before answering this question, one further point requires clarification: when people hear the lections read in a worship setting, do they assume that they are hearing readings from the Bible, or *interpretations* of biblical writings? In my experience, people regard these lections to be *translations* of the Bible. And indeed, I believe this is exactly what they should be, for reasons we shall develop below. If this is the case, in what form should these readings of the Bible be heard? In a form that gives us an authentic flavor of the message within its original setting, even when that flavor gives offence to some of our cherished values, or in a form that sets forth truths whose conformity to our notions is in part achieved through stripping away culturally determined elements?

To answer this question necessitates distinguishing between two essential but often confused aspects of a biblically based understanding of faith, namely, translation and interpretation. We would define a translation as an accurate rendition of the original text in the host language, the preparation of which is guided by the responsibility of the translator(s) not to falsify, but faithfully to represent the original meaning of the text in its historical specificity and particularity. We would define interpretation, on the other hand, as the exposition of the meaning of a text for a contemporary time and place arising within a dialectical movement, guided by an appropriate hermeneutic, between its original meaning and the contemporary setting to which it is being applied. Maintenance of this dialectic depends as much on preservation of the integrity and accuracy of the translation, including a faithful rendition of the milieu which is reflected by the original texts, as it does on commitment to interpreting the Bible in a way that communicates its meaning in a language that avoids all that obstructs, and embraces all that fosters understanding.[2]

As cultural and linguistic changes occur, they necessitate changes in both translation and interpretation, but these changes occur on two different levels. In the case of translation, change occurs only as contemporary cultural and linguistic changes necessitate modifications in order to keep the translation faithful to the historical meaning of the text. In the case of interpretation, change occurs as the result of the cumulative insight gained into God's will from the lively interplay between biblical text and new experiences, insights certainly including those arising from movements dedicated to the removal of structures that lead to the oppression of certain groups of humans, whether those structures be political, social or linguistic.

The theological understanding underlying this distinction between the tasks of translation and interpretation views revelation, truth or meaning not in timeless/mythic terms, but as a process arising from a long historical chain of confessions responding to what is perceived as God's prevenient gracious acts. Since God's presence is experienced and the responses to that presence are formed within the culturally determined concepts and forms of expression of the specific time in question, historical/cultural specificity is an inextricable aspect of this revelatory process. In fact, the dynamic, progressive quality of biblical faith is blurred by attempts to remove historical/cultural-specific aspects. To give one example: the earliest code of law in the Bible, the Book of the Covenant in Exodus 20-23, contains a form of the law governing the release of slaves which is prejudiced against the female slave, in that only the male is entitled to manumission in the seventh year. In the later reformulation of this law in Deuteronomy 15, this prejudice is removed. The inclusiveness of the law is extended even further in the still later formulation found in Leviticus 25, where the enslavement of Hebrew slaves is forbidden entirely. Any attempt to make the Book of the Covenant more inclusive than it is would dull the progressive/dynamic quality of the Bible which becomes evident when the entire canon is considered with each of its parts interpreted within their own specific historical and social settings. Indeed, it is only against the background of the more limited formulations of earlier biblical times that the full theological and social significance of a passage like Galatians 3:28-29 becomes evident: "There is neither Jew nor Greek, there is neither slave nor free, there is neither male nor female; for you are all one in Christ Jesus. And if you are Christ's, then you are Abraham's offspring, heirs according to promise."

The dynamic nature of God's revelation of God's will to humans thus has been preserved at least in part due to the fidelity with which each new generation of the community of faith has preserved its confessional monuments over the ages. In countless cases where the new might have supplanted the old, both were preserved alongside each other, thus giving us the diverse and rich record that we have. For example, the compilers of the Book of Deuteronomy did not replace the earlier formulation of the Torah, but added the new formulation they felt God commanded within their changed situation. Similarly, the writers of the Book of Leviticus did not replace the earlier laws, but again added theirs to the older versions. Similarly, Jesus' words did not supplant the Hebrew Torah, but extended it by means of yet further interpretation (e.g., Matt 5:17-48). In each of these cases, old formulations were found to be inadequate within the changed situations of later generations, but they were nevertheless faithfully preserved and revered for what they were, namely, expressions of God's presence in the historical experiences of ancestors in the faith. As new was thus added to old, tensions arose, and we see evidence of this at every stage of biblical history. But there seems to have been considerable tolerance of such tension, and all of us who have inherited the Bible as our spiritual legacy are the fortunate benefactors of this tolerance.

On the level of translation as well as on the level of interpretation, we can be guided by our biblical ancestors. From their care in preserving the spiritual monuments of the past we can be tutored in handing down faithful translations of our confessional heritage.

From their daring in reformulating the faith so as to apply its dynamic to their changed situation we can be challenged to use our creative imagination to proclaim God's Word in an idiom which is worthy of its contents and in keeping with our best understanding of God's will and presence in our world. And though tensions surely will be felt between the old formulations and the new, they ultimately relate harmoniously to one another, since it is precisely the long history of confessions preserved in their specificity that encourages us to try to keep up with the living God as that God addresses each age anew. To seek to give one normative rendition of that long, variegated tradition by flattening it in conformity with the ideology and taste of our own time could only result in a blurring and a flattening of the history of God's relation with humans.[3]

This lesson applies even in the case of elements of the Bible which in the light of our own understanding of faith are blatantly exclusive, inappropriate and offensive, such as the divine commands to exterminate the enemy in Joshua 6:21, I Samuel 15:2-3 and Deuteronomy 20:16-17, or the words found at the conclusion of the song in Psalm 137. Though the Inclusive-Lectionary Committee has shown considerable restraint in relation to the exclusive aspects of the Hebrew Bible (the instances in increasing the degree of inclusivenes in the New Testament being far more frequent, a distinction reflecting a lingering Marcionite inclination), there is a tendency to blunt the original patriarchal texture of the ancient Israelite society through renditions such as the following: ". . .that you may dwell in the land which God swore to your ancestors, to Abraham [*and Sarah**], to Isaac [*and Rebecca**], and to Jacob, (*and Leah, and Rachel**], to give them." Though the Committee has exercised every caution (through brackets, italics and footnotes) to alert the *reader* to these additions, the one *hearing* the lection within the worship setting will not be able to distinguish the additions from the original. What will this hearer then hear? To put the matter bluntly, she or he will hear a description of the divine promise from a milieu other than the actual patriarchal milieu of ancient Israel. Is this desirable? I do not believe it is, for I believe we should understand the historical confessions of our faith each in its particular form, for only then can we grasp both the rootedness of the divine/human relationship within the specific context of each biblical period and the dynamic movement that characterizes that ongoing relationship.

While no one can deny that all translation involves interpretation, since there is never a one-to-one equivalency between an ancient word or phrase and a contemporary one, restraints such as we have been describing seem to be necessary if importation of personal or in-group theologies, ideologies and social tastes into the translation of the biblical text is to be kept at a minimum. This point can be illustrated by reference to *An Inclusive-Language Lectionary*'s rendition of Matthew 3:1-12. Here John the Baptist's verbal attack on the Pharisees and Sadducees is presented thus:

> You brood of vipers! Who warned you to
> flee from the wrath to come? Bear fruit that
> befits repentance, and do not presume to
> say to yourselves, "We have Abraham as
> our father [*and Sarah and Hagar as our
> mothers**]"; for I tell you, God is able from
> these stones to raise up children to
> Abraham, [*Sarah, and Hagar**].[4]

The intention of the Lectionary Committee is clear: as in the case of the passage from Deuteronomy 30 cited earlier, the exclusive focus on the partriarchs in the Hebrew Bible is broadened to include reference to female ancestors as well. The underlying intention is commendable, but the hazards entailed in introducing elements not in the text are immediately clear. As we indicated earlier, one of the chief responsibilities of the translator is to preserve as precisely as possible both the original meaning and the social milieu of the text. This New Testament text cannot be understood without its background in the promise to Abraham, upon which Israel, and specifically in New Testament times, the Pharisees and Sadducees, based their notion of divine election. Throughout the genealogical narratives and lists of Genesis, this election was transmitted to later generations by a process of selection (interpreted as divine election) which eliminated all offspring except one as bearer of the covenant promise. In the case of Abraham's offspring, one of the lines which was thus excluded was that of Hagar the Egyptian, who bore Abraham the son Ishmael, who according to the biblical genealogical structure, was the eponymous ancestor of a nomadic group of peoples located in North Arabia (cf. Gen 16; 17:18-27; 21:8-21 and 25:12-18).

Though our modern attitudes toward the importance of inclusiveness, both along ethnic and sexual lines, fosters a deep desire to find the roots of these attitudes in Scripture, the temptation to import more inclusiveness into specific passages than is actually there must be restrained. Both out of a sense of fidelity to our textual base which is the benchmark of all translating, and for theological reasons already discussed, we must allow the texts to speak their own message authentically out of their own time. In the case of the Matthean text, no Pharisee or Sadducee, in fact no Jew of biblical times, would claim Hagar as a mother. The notion is historically, ethnographically and theologically absurd. The Jew was carrier of the promise precisely because Hagar had been *excluded* from God's promise to Abraham; or put another way, the Jew bore the Abrahamic promise precisely because his or her mother was not Hagar, but Sarah. This understanding of the Genesis genealogy comes clearly to expression in Paul's allegorical application of the Hagar story in Galatians 4:21-31: whereas the offspring of Sarah are "children of promise," the offspring of Hagar, the slave, are of "the flesh."

Translators of the Bible must strive to place fidelity to the original meaning and context of the biblical text above all personal ideologies and commitments, for to do otherwise is to endanger the autonomy of the Bible's witness. We have no problem affirming this basic principle in the face of Nazi attempts to erase the Jewishness of Jesus, or even the Evangelical's alleged doctrinal motivation for translating *'alma* in Isaiah 7:14 as "virgin" rather than "young woman." Understandably, we find it more difficult to maintain a corresponding detachment from the movements and issues that are theologically most urgent for us. Because I personally feel so committed to reforming our theological language and concepts so as to make them more suitable vehicles of the universal inclusiveness of divine purpose which I see developing out of the long history of our confessional heritage, I feel challenged to explain the issue at stake in our varying approaches to translating the Bible. There is no denying the fact that in the first instance, the more restrained approach to translating produces greater tensions between the biblical text and the interpretation of God's word for today than is the case with an approach which would alter aspects of the original text through considerable interpretative intervention. But the blurring of the historical, social and theological specificity, which to me is an indispensable aspect of all of our confessional monuments, is too high a cost to pay for ameliorating this initial tension. I feel that if we truly grasp the central dynamic of the biblical message within the context of a community of faith where this dynamic is embodied in a viable contemporary form through careful study, disciplined prayer and inspired preaching, each biblical text can be accepted for what it is, that is, *one* specific historical expression of

God's Word to God's people. If each instance of that Word, rather than being forced to stand in isolation as full disclosure of God's Word, is taken as one concrete moment within the broad context of the canon and of the entire history of God's relating to God's people, we will not need to whitewash away any of the often glaring marks of our ancestors' partial vision, for they testify to their limited attempts to embody their vision of God's will in the particular historical, social and liguistic vehicles available to them.[5] We shall rather be grateful for their partial contributions to the whole picture which is yet unfolding, and rejoice that we, as we struggle to find more adequate ways to describe the Ineffable, are also a part of that unfolding.

Footnotes

1. *An Inclusive Language Lectionary* (Published for the Cooperative Publication Association by John Knox Press, Atlanta, The Pilgrim Press, New York and The Westminster Press, Philadelphia, *Readings for the Year A*, 1983, *Readings for the Year B*, 1984, *Readings for the Year C*, 1985).

2. For a fuller treatment of this hermeneutic, cf. the "Appendix" in P. D. Hanson, *The People Called: The Growth of Community in the Bible* (New York and San Francisco: Harper & Row, 1986).

3. This point is stated clearly by Lucetta Mowry in the "Commentary" section of the September 3, 1982 edition of the *Christian Science Monitor*: ". . .translators by catering to the preferences and prejudices of special interest groups will satisfy the religious, moral and social needs of a limited number of people."

4. Advent 2, *Readings for Year A*. It is noteworthy that in the *Readings for Year B* and *Readings for Year C*, in passages where female figures are added to the text, Hagar no longer is included, perhaps reflecting a conscious change of policy by the Inclusive-Lectionary Committee.

5. "In all religious traditions people make a distinction between the ultimate basis upon which they build their personal faith and the way others before them have expressed it. In the Christian tradition we accept the biblical expression as traditional, for we live not to ourselves alone but by the increment of all that persons throughout the centuries have held to be true and sacred." Lucetta Mowry in the article cited in footnote 3.

JAMES LUTHER MAYS
A BIBLIOGRAPHY
Compiled by John B. Trotti

1957   "The Faithfulness of God in Amos and Hosea." Ph.D. dissertation, University of Manchester, 1957.

1959   *The Book of Leviticus; Numbers* (The Layman's Bible Commentary, Vol. 4). Richmond: John Knox Press, 1959.

       "Words About the Words of Amos: Recent Study of the Book of Amos." *Interpretation*, XIII (July, 1959), 259-72

1960   *Exegesis as a Theological Discipline.* Richmond, Va.: Union Theological Seminary, 1960. Also "Exegesis as a Theological Discipline." [Phototape] Richmond, Va.: Union Theological Seminary Library. Inaugural address presented April 20, 1960.

       "God Has Spoken: A Meditation on Genesis 12:1-4." *Interpretation*, XIV (October, 1960), 413-20.

       Review of *Interpreting the Bible*, by J. C. K. von Hofman, *Interpretation*, XIV (April, 1960), 211-14.

1961   (Translator). Noth, Martin. "'Re-presentation' of the Old Testament in Proclamation." *Interpretation*, XV (January, 1961), 50-60.

1962   Review of *Theology of the Old Testament*, Vol. I, by Walther Eichrodt. *Theology Today*, XIX (October, 1962), 430-34.

1963   (Translation editor). Westermann, C. ed. *Essays on Old Testament Interpretation*. English translation edited by J. L. Mays. London: SCM Press, 1963.

1965   "Epistle from a Present-day Apostle." *Presbyterian Survey* (June, 1965), 26-28.

1966   "Editorial." *Interpretation*, XX (January, 1966), 78-80; (April, 1966),229-30.

1969   *Amos; A Commentary*, (Old Testament Library). Philadelphia: Westminster Press, 1969. (also London: SCM Press, 1969.)

       Hosea; A Commentary, (Old Testament Library). Philadelphia: Westminster Press, 1969. (also London: SCM Press, 1969.)

       "Worship, World, and Power: An Interpretation of Psalm 100." *Interpretation*, XXIII (July, 1969), XXIII 315-30.

       "Editorial." *Interpretation*, XXIII (January, 1969), 78-80; (April, 1969): 218-19; (July, 1969): 331-32; (October, 1969): 466-67.

1970   "Editorial." *Interpretation* XXIV (January, 1970): 92-93; (April, 1970): 131-38; (July, 1970): 357-58; (October, 1970): 510-11.

1971   "Editorial." *Interpretation* XXV (January, 1971): 3-10; (April, 1971): 194; (July, 1971): 345-46; (October, 1971): 500-01.

1972   "Jesus Came Preaching: A Study and Sermon on Mark 1:14-15." *Interpretation* XXVI (January, 1972): 30-41.

       "On Building Babylon, Genesis 11:1-9." Thesis Theological Cassettes, 3:7 (August, 1972). 15 minutes.

       "Song for Celebration, Psalm 133." Thesis Theological Cassettes, 3:2 (March, 1972). 12 minutes.

"Editorial." *Interpretation*, XXVI(January, 1972): 72-73; (April, 1972): 210-11; (July, 1972). 338-40; (October, 1972): 469-70.

1973   "Widening Circle of Redemption, Mark 1:40-45." Thesis Theological Cassettes, 3:12 (January, 1973). 13 minutes.

"Editorial." *Interpretation*, XXVII (January, 1973): 86-87; (April, 1973): 203-04; (July, 1973): 349-50; (October, 1973): 387-88.

1974   "Power to Forgive, Mark 2:1-12." Thesis Theological Cassettes, 4:12 (January, 1974). 14½ minutes.

"Editorial." *Interpretation*, XXVIII (January, 1974): 89-90; (April, 1974): 131-32; (October, 1974): 458-59.

1975   "Editorial." *Interpretation*, XXIX (January, 1975), 73-74.

"Introduction to 'The History of Israel and Biblical Faith.'" *Interpretation*, XXIX (April, 1975), 115-17.

"Editorial." *Interpretation*, XXIX (July, 1975), 239-94; (October 1975): 422-23.

1976   "An Exposition of Mark 8:27 - 9:1." *Interpretation*, XXX (April, 1976), 174-78.

"Historical and Canonical: Recent Discussion About the Old Testament and Christian Faith." *Magnalia Dei: The mighty Acts of God: Essays on the Bible and Archaeology in Memory of G. Ernest Wright*, pp. 510-28. Edited by Frank Moore Cross, Werner E. Lemke and Patrick D. Miller. Garden City, NY: Doubleday & Company, 1976.

Micah; A Commentary (Old Testament Library). Philadelphia: Westminster Press, 1976. (also London: SCM Press, 1976.)

"Editorial." *Interpretation*, XXX (April, 1976), 184-85; (July, 1976): 297-98; (October, 1976): 410-11.

1977   "Theological Purpose of the Book of Micah." In *Beiträge zur Alttestamentlichen Theologie: Festschrift fur Walther Zimmerli Zum 70*. Geburtstag pp. 276-87. Edited by Herbert Donner, Robert Hanhart and Rudolph Smend. Göttingen: Vandenhoek & Reprecht, 1977.

"Editorial." *Interpretation* XXXI (April, 1977), 179-80; (July, 1977): 291-92; (October, 1977): 410-11.

1978   *Ezekiel, Second Isaiah* (Proclamation Commentaries). Philadelphia: Fortress Press, 1978.

"He Goes Before You: A Chapel Meditation on Mark 16:1-8." *As I See It Today*, 8:6 (June, 1978).

"Herbert Gordon May (1904-1977)." *Zeitschrift für die Alttestamentliche Wissenschaft*, 90:3 (1978), 111-14.

". . .And She Served Them: Reflections on Mark 1:29-31." *As I See It Today*, 9:2 (November, 1978).

"Editorial." *Interpretation* XXXII (January, 1978), 84-85; (April, 1978): 185-86; (July, 1978): 301-02; (October, 1978): 414-15.

Review of *Joel and Amos: A Commentary on the Books of the Prophets Joel and Amos*, by Hans Walter Wolff in *Interpretation*, XXXII (July, 1978.), 314-16.

1979   "What is Man: Reflections on Psalm 8." *From Faith to Faith*: Essays in Honor of Donald G. Miller on his Seventieth Birthday, pp. 203-18. Edited by Dikran Y. Hadidian. Pittsburgh: Pickwick Press, 1979.

"Editorial." *Interpretation*, XXXIII (January, 1979), 73-74; (April, 1979): 188-89; (July, 1979): 299-300; (October 1979): 404-05.

Review of *Understanding the Old Testament*, by A. H. J. Gunneweg. *Interpretation*, XXXIII (October, 1979), 406-10.

1980   "Psalm 13." An Expository Article. *Interpretation*, XXXIV (July, 1980), 279-83.

"What is Written: A Response to Brevard Childs' *Introduction to the Old Testament as Scripture*." *Horizons in Biblical Theology*, 2 (1980), 151-63.

"Editorial." *Interpretation*, XXXIV (January, 1980), 75-76; (April 1980): 182-83; (July 1980): 227-28; (October 1980): 339-40.

Review of *Old Testament Theology: A Fresh Approach*, by Ronald E. Clements. *Journal of Biblical Literature*, 99 (September, 1980), 442,444.

Review of *A Commentary on the Book of the Prophet Ezekiel, Chapters 1 - 24* by Walther Zimmerli. *Interpretation*, XXXIV (October, 1980), 426-430.

1981   *Interpreting the Gospels*. Edited by James Luther Mays. Philadelphia: Fortress Press, 1981.

"Editorial." *Interpretation*, XXXV (January, 1981), 3-4; (April, 1981): 115-16; (July 1981): 227-28; (October 1981): 339-40.

1982   "Response to Janzen: 'Metaphor and Reality in Hosea 11.'" *Semeia*, 24 (1982), 45-51.

(Editor) Walter Brueggemann, *Genesis*. (Interpretation: The Bible Commentary for Teaching and Preaching), James L. Mays, Series Editor, Patrick D. Miller, Old Testament Editor. Atlanta: John Knox Press, 1982.

(Editor) Charles Cousar, *Galatians*. (Interpretation: The Bible Commentary for Teaching and Preaching), James L. Mays, Series Editor, Paul J. Achtemeier, New Testament Editor. Atlanta: John Knox Press, 1982.

"Editorial." *Interpretation*, XXXVI (January, 1982), 3-4; (April, 1982): 115-16; (July, 1982): 227-28; (October, 1982): 339-40.

1983   "Justice: Perspectives from the Prophetic Tradition." *Interpretation*, XXXVII (January, 1983), 5-17.

(Editor) Lamar Williamson, *Mark.*. (Interpretation: A Bible Commentary for Teaching and Preaching), James L. Mays, Series Editor, Paul J. Achtemeier, New Testament Editor. Atlanta: John Knox Press, 1983.

"Editorial." *Interpretation*, XXXVII (January, 1983), 3-4; (April, 1983): 115-16; (July, 1983): 227-28; (October, 1983): 339.

Review of *Zwölf Propheten: Hosea, Joel, Amos* by Alfons Deissler. *Journal of Biblical Literature*, 102 (September, 1983), 477.

1984   (Editor) Fred Craddock, *Philippians*. (Interpretation: A Bible Commentary for Teaching and Preaching). James L. Mays, Series Editor, Paul J. Achtemeier, New Testament Editor. Atlanta: John Knox Press, 1984.

(Editor) W. Sibley Towner, *Daniel*. (Interpretation: A Bible Commentary for Teaching and Preaching). James L. Mays, Series Editor, Patrick D. Miller, Old Tetament Editor. Atlanta: John Knox Press, 1984,

1985   "Prayer and Christology: Psalm 22 as Perspective on the Passion," *Theology Today* (October, 1985):322-31.

"Psalm 29." An Expository Article. *Interpretation 39 (January, 1985): 60-64*.

(Editor) Paul Achtemeier, *Romans*. (Interpretation: A Bible Commentary for Teaching and Preaching). James L. Mays, editor. Atlanta: John Knox Press, 1985.

(Editor) J. Gerald, *Job*. (Interpretation: A Bible Commentary for Teaching and

Preaching). James L. Mays, Series Editor, Patrick D. Miller, Old Testament Editor. Atlanta: John Knox Press, 1985.

Review of *The Psalms of the Sons of Korah*, by Michael D. Goulder. *Journal of Biblical Literature*, 104 (June, 1985), 318-19.

Review of *A History of Prophecy in Israel: From the Settlement in the Land to the Hellenistic Period*, by Joseph Blenkinsopp, *Interpretation* 30 (October, 1985): 414-16.

1986   "The David of the Psalms, *Interpretation 40 (April, 1986)*:143-155.

CONTRIBUTORS

John H. Leith, Pemberton Professor of Theology, Union Theological Seminary, Richmond, Virginia.

James Barr, Regius Profesor of Hebrew, The University of Oxford, Oxford, England.

Claus Westermann, Emeritus Professor of Old Testament, The University of Heidelberg, Heidelberg, Germany.

Roland S. Clements, Samuel Davidson Professor of Old Testament Studies, King's College, London, England.

Brevard S. Childs, Professor of Old Testament, The Divinity School, Yale University, New Haven, Connecticut.

Roland E. Murpny, O. Carm., Professor of Old Testament, The Divinity School, Duke University, Durham, North Carolina.

Elizabeth Achtemeier, Visiting Professor of Bible and Homiletics, Union Theological Seminary, Richmond, Virginia.

F. Wellford Hobbie, Benjamin Rice Lacy, Jr., Professor of Pastoral Leadership and Homiletics, Union Theological Seminary, Richmond, Virginia.

Patrick D. Miller, Jr., Charles T. Haley Professor of Old Testament Theology, Princeton Theological Seminary, Princeton, New Jersey.

James A. Sanders, President, Ancient Biblical Manuscript Center, Claremont, California.

Paul D. Hanson, Bussey Professor of Divinity, The Divinity School, Harvard University, Cambridge, Massachusetts.

John B. Trotti, Librarian and Henry Muller Brimm, Professor of Bibliography, Union Theological Seminary, Richmond, Virginia.

CONGRATULATORY LIST

J. E. Arnette, Rocky Mount, NC
David R. Bauer, Wilmore, KY
Christopher Begg, Washington, DC
Stephen W. Berghaus, Durham, NC
H. J. H. Bossers, New Castle, PA
Richard & Kathleen Boyce, Bedford, VA
Mr. & Mrs. Robert B. Boyd, Athens, TN
John M. Bracke, Ballwin, MO
Walter Brueggemann, Decatur, GA
Gerald Butler, Beltsville, MD
Mrs. O. B. Cannon, Jr., Louisville, GA
Richard P. Carlson, Roseau, MN
Daniel S. Clark, Rockbridge Baths, VA
Bob Collins, Mexico, MO
Donald E. Gowan, Allison Park, PA
Murray Joseph Haar, Sioux Falls, SD
David G. Hagstrom, Mt. Vernon, SD
Max Harris, White Bear Lake, MN
George C. Heider, Seward, NE
P. Keith Hill, Winnfield, LA
Marc Jolley, Louisville, KY
Ray C. Jones, Jr., Richmond, VA
Jack Dean Kingsbury, Richmond, VA
John S. Kselman, Washington, DC
Wallis D. Landrum, Mexico, MO
Joseph T. Lewis, Richmond, VA
Hector MacLean, Lumberton, NC
Mrs. Ruth M. Mays, Louisville, GA
Yoshifumi Namba, Covina, CA
Frank C. Norris, Wilmore, KY
Terrence Prendergast, S.J., Toronto, Canada
Wayne E. Reeves, Oxford, England
K. R. Salo, Swan River, MB, Canada
Frank L. Seaman, San Antonio, TX
Daud H. Soesilo, Richmond, VA
C. Fitzhugh Spragins, Batesville, AR
The Librarian, Theology Library, Pusey House, Oxford, England
Sibley Towner, Kilmarnock, VA
J. Michael Walker, Tarkio, MO
Marsha M. Wilfong, Richmond, VA
Patrick J. Willson, Midland, TX
Ronald D. Witherup, S.S., Washington, DC
William P. Wood, Charlotte, NC